Lord, Don't Let It Rain At Recess

Lord, Don't Let It Rain At Recess

Devotions For Teachers

PATRICIA ANN FISHER

Daybreak Books

Zondervan Publishing House
Grand Rapids, Michigan

Requests for information should be addressed to:
Zondervan Publishing House
Grand Rapids, Michigan 49530

Lord, Don't Let It Rain at Recess
Copyright © 1988 by Patricia Ann Fisher

Library of Congress Cataloging in Publication Data

Fisher, Patricia Ann.
    Lord, don't let it rain at recess.

    1. Teachers—Prayer-books and devotions—English.
I. Title.
BV4596.T43F57   1988   242'.68   88-103
ISBN 0-310-44521-3

All Scripture quotations, unless otherwise noted, are taken from The Holy Bible: New
International Version (North American Edition), copyright © 1973, 1978, 1984 by the
International Bible Society. Used by permission of Zondervan Bible Publishers.

Edited and designed by Julie Ackerman Link

Printed in the United States of America

93 94 95 / CH / 15 14   13 12 11 10

Through the grace of God we have different gifts. . . .
if it is teaching, let us give all we have to our teaching.
Romans 12:6–7 (Phillips)

Contents

Preface

There is no way I could be a teacher without constant prayer—an ongoing conversation with God. Many other teachers have told me that they feel the same. It was with their encouragement (and nagging!) that this book was written. It is for them— they know who they are. A few I must list for special encouragement: Verna, Selby and Shirley, Pat, Cindy, Rose, Mary Lou, Norma, Susie, Agnes and the aides. A special thank you for Amanda, my very own Mary Poppins. May the Lord continue to bless their teaching (and mine!).

Finally, I'd like to thank Julie Ackerman Link for her humor, grace, and encouragement during the editing of this book. Bon Voyage. God go with you.

BEGINNINGS

*A*nother long sunburnt summer is over, and once again it is time for school to begin.

I steer my ancient car through a maze of strewn glass and into its accustomed parking place. As I rest my head against the steering wheel for a moment, my thoughts go back twenty-five years to the Midwest.

With a crisp, new teaching credential clutched in my hand, I arrived to prepare for the first day of class expecting to see the school where I had interviewed that spring. Instead I found ashes and rubble, the result of a massive fire that had destroyed the school. In dismay and near panic I found the nearest pay phone and called the principal.

"With the grace of God and a few portable classrooms we'll make it," he said. "And soon you'll get to teach in a brand new school," he promised.

Some teachers with seniority did get portable classrooms. But not me. I got a shed that formerly housed janitorial supplies. When the fall rains came, my students and I waded through mud that oozed over our shoes. When the winter snows came, I had to arrive early to stoke up an old potbellied stove, our sole source of heat.

The fire had claimed all our supplies, including textbooks

and the ditto machine, so we were forced back to frontier-type teaching—a chalkboard, pencils, and paper were my only teaching aids. (The state promised all year to rush us emergency supplies, but apparently they didn't know where we were—after all, it was a very large state, and they had only 185 days to find us.)

It *was* by the grace of God that I made it through that year. Each day I found refuge in the Psalms. I read them when I awoke, during breaks in the school day, and again before collapsing at night. First-year teaching weariness, compounded by a less-than-ideal teaching situation, made me cling to Psalm 91 as tenaciously as a small child clings to a mother's hand. I prayed myself through that year.

By the time a new school had been constructed, Psalm 91, constant prayer, and frontier conditions had become an intrinsic part of my style of teaching. My philosophy didn't fit a new school, so I left to find one that needed me.

Now, some twenty-five years later, I squint my eyes and try to view Adams School objectively. Like the surrounding neighborhood, it is ancient and dilapidated. Some call it a barrio school, some a ghetto school, all a poverty school.

I see these things, too, Lord, but I feel the leap of excitement of a new school year, the anticipation of things yet to come. And beyond that, I feel that this is home, a place that tugs at my heart, a place where I belong. Above all, this is a place of love. Help me to remember this moment, Lord, when the children can't seem to learn and I can't seem to teach, when my job seems overwhelming and useless. Help me in those times to touch this moment of love, to find it when I need it most. Sustain me in your love, Lord, I pray.

I allow myself one last sigh, gather my books in my arms, slam the car door, and head for my classroom. Another school year has begun.

HE WHO DWELLS IN THE SHELTER OF THE MOST
HIGH WILL REST IN THE SHADOW OF THE ALMIGHTY

(PSALM 91:1).

FRONTIER TEACHING

*M*aybe this will be the year I don't survive the first day. I worry about it every year. I have thirty-two first-graders again. That's a lot of them all at once, and the problems seem overwhelming. Suzanne, her blond braids swinging to emphasize every word, never stops talking. She's going to need clearly defined and firmly set limits. I should do it today, but Denny, the little blond with the vacant look, is lost somewhere between the bathroom and our classroom. We put out a full-scale alert and finally locate him back in the kindergarten room, where he probably should have stayed. And Juan is lying on the floor. His cumulative record shows that he spent all last year on the floor too.

Lord, I'm going to need help with these children, especially Juan. Bodies lying in the middle of the room distract me. And by the way, why does it always have to be 100° on the first day of school? And why doesn't the evaporative cooler work? And why can't schools have air conditioning? And why does water just trickle from drinking fountains, defying efforts to get even a sip of lukewarm water? And why won't the windows open?

I feel as if I start every year praying for the wrong things— a slight breeze, recess, and three o'clock. I remind myself once again that I chose frontier teaching. Furthermore, I am beginning to think that all caring teachers are frontier teachers. Frontier teaching demands that teachers have high expectations for each student. No child, whether from the ghetto, barrio, or even the "right" side of town, will ever realize his or her highest potential unless someone expects it. I know it's unrealistic to expect it all the first day, and I'm tired and my feet hurt and my head aches. Right now I just want to go home.

Finally it is three o'clock, and I turn thirty-two exhausted youngsters free. The first day is not easy for them either.

Thank you, Lord, for take-out pizza, sofas, pillows, and peace.

NEVER BE LACKING IN ZEAL, BUT KEEP YOUR SPIRITUAL FERVOR, SERVING THE LORD (ROMANS 12:11).

SECOND THOUGHTS

When the morning bell rings, I feel elated that my class has the straightest line on the playground. And when we enter the classroom, everyone sits quietly, hands folded, waiting expectantly. Everyone, that is, except Juan, who is back on the floor.

I decide that this is the day Juan will learn to sit at a desk. "Juan," I say, "we're going to learn many new things this year. We're going to learn to read, to write, to do math, and to draw. So you will need pencils, papers, and beautiful new crayons. And I'm sure you'll need a desk to hold all these new things."

Pleased with myself for sounding so self-assured, I wait for Juan to get up and move to his desk. But Juan stares through me with total disinterest and finally buries his head in his arms. My smugness gone, I add firmly, "Juan, I need you at your desk." Nothing. Maybe if I physically set him at the desk he'll stay, I think. But he is a mass of limp arms and legs. I may as well try to mold jello into a sitting position. I look at the clock. It is only 8:35, and already I've lost a major battle.

Lord, why do I always forget that the second day of school is never much better than the first?

I try to get the rest of the class into learning groups. One thing is certain: there's plenty of room at the top! I won't have to worry about running out of things to teach. This is the worst class

I've had yet—kids in the lowest group aren't even sure of their own names. Denny can't find his way across the room without getting lost, and Todd wet his pants because he forgot where the bathroom is.

Oops. I guess I belong with the low group. I forgot playground duty. Kate, the second-grade teacher, yells in the door at recess time. "You forgot playground duty. There are 150 kids out there with no one to supervise them." I hurry out, thinking how ridiculous it is for anyone to think that one adult can make much difference.

Lord, help me remember that one person can make a difference. You did, and I'm here because I believe I can too, with your help.

GIVE EAR TO MY WORDS, O LORD, CONSIDER MY SIGHING (PSALM 5:1).

CAFETERIA CHAOS

*T*oday I have lunch duty. I must be good at repressing memories of it, because I am continually amazed at how miserable it is to spend the lunch hour in a crowded, noisy cafeteria with 600 children doing everything but eating.

We have a rule in our cafeteria: no conversing with your neighbor. No one breaks this rule ever. Conversing with a neighbor would be calm stuff. Most children scream across the room. And if the principal enters the cafeteria during lunch, she'll judge me on my ability to keep 600 children quiet, even though I don't know 568 of them. Fortunately, few administrators venture into cafeterias during lunchtime, lest their own disciplinary abilities be judged!

In addition to the noise, there is mess. Lunch pails depicting every Saturday cartoon are slung carelessly over the tables, contents spilled out recklessly. Parents who fill lunch pails come in two basic types. The first type assumes the child will have to plow the south forty before noon. They send along two bulky sandwiches, a bag of chips, an orange, an apple, a bunch of grapes, and two cupcakes. The child eats the cupcakes and dumps the rest. The other type of parent just sends two cupcakes, which the child greedily devours while his eyes never leave the sandwiches that the other child is about to throw away. But we do not allow children to share food. In fact, the rule is so rigidly enforced that it belongs among the cardinal rules of education at our school.

Lord, something is wrong when we teach children that it is better to throw away food than to share it. Maybe, just maybe, teaching children about world hunger should start in school cafeterias, with the person seated next to each child. Perhaps then the children in Africa would seem more real. I think the chaos in the cafeteria does not all belong to the students.

THE MAN WITH TWO TUNICS SHOULD SHARE WITH
HIM WHO HAS NONE, AND THE ONE WHO HAS FOOD
SHOULD DO THE SAME (LUKE 3:11).

A PLACE FOR JUAN

*A*fter spending an hour in a cafeteria with 600 children, coming back to a room with only thirty-two seems like moving to easy street, even with Juan still on the floor.

Today I am prepared for the heat. It's nearly 100 degrees, but I have a cold, wet paper towel for each perspiring little face and ice water in a thermos I brought from home for each parched throat.

As the children rest their heads on their desks, I turn on Beethoven's *Pastoral* and try to help them with imagery. "Think about a soft green field and a bright blue sky with just a few tufts of soft, cottony clouds drifting by," I suggest. "It's very peaceful and still." A few quiet minutes of reflection will stimulate their imaginations, give them ideas and feelings of their own, and stir within them a need to communicate. But the children do not yet know my plan; they are simply relieved to have a few moments to rest before the afternoon begins.

During the afternoon I try to determine who can count. Some day we'll know enough numbers to count the jellybeans in the jar on my desk. Then we'll count each color separately and make graphs to correspond to each color. But for now I let each child guess the number of jellybeans. Javier guesses four million, Suzanne six, and Michael ninety-eight. He is very nearly correct.

Later, from the same jar, we'll count gumdrops, gumballs, marbles, and anything else I can find to encourage a first-grader's enthusiasm about numbers. We'll discuss favorite flavors of ice cream and make graphs to show preferences. Then one very special day in the spring we'll visit the ice cream store a block from school and complete our math lesson over huge ice cream cones. Most will be chocolate, but bubble gum usually runs a close second.

The air in the room has become stifling. It's time for a break, but the tree-barren playground offers little respite from the heat. "Trade you," offers Shelly, the other first-grade teacher. "You take my kids for recess when I have cafeteria duty and I'll take yours when you do."

Bless her, Lord. I head for what is left from the lunch I didn't get time to eat, but curiosity gets the best of me and I stop at the office to take a closer look at Juan's folder. "Immature, lies on floor—6/82—retained." The following year a note from the school psychologist adds, "Visited home; no one else lies on floor. Who knows?" And a final note from the despairing teacher, "Immature, lies on floor—6/83—passed to first grade." This was all the information we had gained in two years about a little boy named Juan. *Lord, help me find a way to reach this little one of yours.*

Toward the end of the day, the children help me pass out eight forms per child for parents to complete by the following day. Every year we send home these forms to find out important information, like which parents will help with parties and which ones allow their children to go on field trips, and every year approximately ninety percent are lost or converted into paper airplanes. The next day I'll send home eight more forms to replace those that were lost. Eventually, due to persistence and an unlimited supply of forms, I'll complete my file on each student. In the meantime, though, we'll have wasted enough paper for a ticker-tape parade down main street. This year I'm giving stickers to students who return their forms. It increases my chances for success.

In the closing moments of school, I help the children review the day. "What was happiest for you today?" I ask them.

"I liked it that we're going to read," Jason replies, eyes shining.

"I liked the music," Wendy volunteers.

"Lunch. I liked lunch," adds Javier. The free cafeteria lunch Javier consumed would probably be his only meal for the day. No wonder it made him so happy.

"What made you feel unhappy?" I ask.

Denny's arm waves wildly, "I don't like getting lost all the time." I jot a note to myself: "Try to keep from losing Denny."

Bright-eyed Julia asks, "Why does Juan lie on the floor all the time? I don't like that." Neither does the teacher, but I can't let on that it upsets me.

Just before I dismiss the class, I ask, "Juan, could you stay after school for just a minute?" His dark lashes cover his eyes as he lowers them to avoid an encounter.

"For just a minute," he replies as he buries his face in his arms and turns over on his stomach.

As the rest of the class leaves, I unlock the door to the storage room and drag out an old refrigerator box. Lugging it to the back door of the room, I push it outside. "Now, Juan, I want you to hold on to this box. I'm going to get a hammer and some nails."

I return with my tools and begin hammering a nail to attach the cardboard box to the back door.

"What're you doing?" Juan asks, curiosity conquering shyness.

"Building on to the room for more space," I answer as I continue to hammer.

"How come?" he persists, now fairly certain it involves him.

"Well, we're pretty crowded now, and we'll be learning more things and will need even more space. So we won't have room for someone to lie on the floor. This will give you your very own room."

"But it'll be hot out here. And in the winter it will get cold and the rain will come in," he protests.

"Oh, I'll fix it up," I promise. "I'll put a little rug on the floor and everything."

He surveys the box skeptically while I go on hammering. "Mrs. Fisher, I could sit at a desk like the other kids," he finally offers.

"Oh, no. You'll like this, Juan," I assure him. "Just wait until it's finished."

"I want my own desk; I don't want this old hot box," he argues.

"Are you absolutely sure, Juan?" I ask. "Out here you can lie down."

I look around for Juan, but he is already seated at his desk with his hands folded.

"I'll tell you what. I'll put the box away for a little while. We can always get it out again."

Juan nods in agreement as he helps me tug the box back into storage. "Bye, Mrs. Fisher," he grins as he turns toward the door.

"Bye, see you tomorrow," I answer.

Suddenly he races back, throws his arms around my neck, and then, just as quickly, turns and races from the room.

Thank you, Lord, for helping me find a place to begin with Juan. And don't let me forget that it is just that—a beginning. And as for me, Lord, it is definitely time for hamburgers-to-go and time to hear about the school adventures of my own five children.

I head for my car with a load of books in one arm and my shoes in the other.

FOR THE LORD GIVES WISDOM, AND FROM HIS
MOUTH COME KNOWLEDGE AND UNDERSTANDING
(PROVERBS 2:6).

READING YARNS

*B*efore I became a teacher I never gave much thought to yarn, but now I know it is a necessary ingredient for teaching kindergarten and first grade. Each year I make yarn necklaces in four different colors—approximately eight each of red, yellow, blue, and green, the colors children usually learn to recognize first. I laugh at the absurdity of this ritual, but at least it helps children identify their assigned group at the beginning of the year.

Some teachers identify groups in other ways, frequently with animal names, claiming that colors indicate a lack of creativity on the part of the teacher. But when these teachers use names like turtles, snails, elephants, and blue jays, I wonder what child could be expected to progress very rapidly as a turtle or a snail. Now a blue jay—those are the children who will soar. I have no difficulty identifying the slow groups, and I suspect that even a first-grader can figure it out.

So I stick with colors. I hold up the necklaces and am relieved to discover that all the children can identify them, even Juan (who is still at a desk). Taking nothing for granted, I again ask each child what color necklace he or she has, and again I'm rewarded with thirty-two correct answers. But then I make a fatal error. Pointing to the place where I have laid out ten work sheets, I ask, "Will everyone with a red necklace come to this table? Only red necklaces," I emphasize.

Instantly I am mobbed by thirty-two first-graders. I'd forgotten that in first grade going anywhere beats staying put. No matter what color your necklace is!

"All right, everyone sit down," I begin again, trying to keep my voice sounding calm and patient while inside I am stomping furiously and kicking the wall. "Raise your hand if you have a red necklace." The appropriate ten hands go up. "Good. Now just those people come to this table." This time it works better. I get only eleven children at the table. I send Denny back to his seat. Then Wendy, with more care and patience than I'll ever possess, gets up and shows him where it is. *Lord, thank you for the Wendys you send along every year. I guess you know how much I need them.*

I finally get the children divided into reading groups. Angela, Wendy, Katie, Lisa, Todd, and Jason were already beginning to read when they came into first grade. But Juan, Denny, Candy, Suzanne, and Michelle are still learning that the abstract figures I call letters have meanings. In between are two groups of average or slightly above average children who will learn to read this year, but only after considerable tugging and pushing by all of us.

Basically, I'm a phonics person, so that's where I begin. If basic phonic instruction is lacking, later on, in second or third grade, a child will have no method or framework for decoding unfamiliar words. So most textbooks and teachers start with short vowel sounds, which generate such intriguing reading material as this: The fat cat sat on a hat. The fat rat sat on a hat. The fat bat sat on a hat. As Angela commented, "That hat must have been a real mess!" With such taut, gripping sentences, it's amazing that I can ever pull students away from their reading groups.

Yet even with such boring material, six-year-olds approach reading with great eagerness. Maybe some of them see parents or older siblings reading. Maybe they know their teacher loves reading. Maybe they realize that books can take them to intriguing places. But whatever the reason, whether learned or intuitive, reading teachers should take full advantage of it because it doesn't last forever. Children can lose it quickly and unexpectedly, and many of them lose it at school.

I always worry most about the lowest reading group. Often immature, they also represent learning problems that probably never will be adequately diagnosed and physical problems, such as inadequate vision and hearing, which should be diagnosed long before first grade but seldom are.

Then there is the child who simply does not learn. Often the child is passed from grade to grade by teachers who try their best but fail to unlock the barriers to learning. And if that child is retained, then what? He or she will usually do better the next year; after all it is a rerun. But the year after that often finds the child in the same situation, only one year older. We tell parents, "Your child cannot learn," but in reality, the hard, cruel fact is that we do not know how to teach that child.

Lord, I realize I cannot solve all their problems, but help me reach each of these children in some way that can make a difference.

THEREFORE, SINCE THROUGH GOD'S MERCY WE HAVE THIS MINISTRY, WE DO NOT LOSE HEART (2 CORINTHIANS 4:1).

WHAT A DRILL!

W hile lost in thoughts about phonics, reading groups, and slow learners, I feel a slow roll under my feet. I remember that I should have talked about earthquakes the very first day of school, when we all could have been calm about it. It is too late now. I look out over a sea of small faces awaiting my reaction.

What I say comes out very carefully. "This is an earthquake drill. Everyone get under your desk, quickly and quietly." They react in an orderly way, assuming I'm in control. The rolling continues, only a bit more viciously. I realize I should be under my desk, too, but considering the debris, both on it and in it, I conclude that a falling ceiling would be less likely to cause injury.

In the midst of the rolling, my curiosity gets the best of me and I start wondering whether the earthquake has a Mammouth or a Coalinga epicenter. Then, in typical teacher style, I think about how I can use the episode later in the day in my teaching.

Although it's very quiet in the room, I sense that panic could take over at any second. "The best place to be at the moment is under your desk with your arms over your head," I say to reassure them. "Denny is doing fine. Suzanne is great. Wendy is doing a good job." My voice drones on calmly, even though I don't feel that way myself.

Lord, don't let me show the fear that is creeping within me. Be with us, Lord, and protect us.

The rolling finally stops. "All right, everyone line up quietly and quickly." Even though building inspectors have assured us that Adams School meets state earthquake standards, I'm not convinced it would take much of an earthquake to do major damage to the ancient building. With this in mind, I make sure the children are outside before the aftershock. We meet other classes filing out; I am not the only one concerned about our elderly school.

Olivia, the sixth-grade teacher, breaks the tension of the moment by blowing her whistle and yelling, "Okay, everybody knows 'I've Been Working on the Railroad,' let's sing." Immediately hands wave from each class to request favorite songs. In a moment, the children have forgotten the earthquake in favor of a singalong.

Later, Peter asks, "How do they do earthquake drills?" I admit that it was a real earthquake and that I'd forgotten to tell them what to do, but didn't want them to be afraid.

"We weren't, were we?" asks Jason with pride in his eyes.

"No, you weren't. You were just super! I was proud of all of you." I realize then that I won't ever climb under my desk because that would frighten them, and one of them might crawl out and get hurt. For sure it would be Denny!

Lord, thank you for the faith these little ones show me. Help me to be worthy of it. Be near to us in all our times of need.

HE REPLIED, "YOU OF LITTLE FAITH, WHY ARE YOU SO AFRAID?" THEN HE GOT UP AND REBUKED THE WINDS AND THE WAVES, AND IT WAS COMPLETELY CALM (MATTHEW 8:26).

THIRTY-ONE

*T*he temperature today is 102 degrees. I debate whether or not to have recess, but the temperature inside is 95 and the children are squirming at their desks. Vacant stares have replaced their usual eager faces. A five- or ten-minute break might help.

"Don't run, boys and girls," I tell them. "Swing or use the slide or sit under the oak tree." It's not really our oak tree; our schoolyard has no trees or shade of any kind. But a huge valley oak stands in a neighboring yard, separated from us by a fence. A few of its majestic branches reach over the fence and provide a patch of shade. "And be sure to get a drink of water," I add, thinking of my empty thermos and the trickle of lukewarm water at the school fountain.

After recess I decide that the patch of shade the oak offers is cooler than our classroom, so we stay outside. Under leafy, breeze-touched branches, I read to the children the latest antics of *Ramona*. The children stretch out on the ground, some lying back to study the soft green leaves, others sitting attentively Indian-style. It's a peaceful moment, until something compels me to count bodies. One is missing. Immediately I know it is Denny.

I announce firmly to the other children, "Everyone stay

here and rest a moment. I need to find Denny. Remember, I'll know who is resting because I'll be able to see you from the school."

Please, Lord, don't let anyone else get lost while I'm gone.

I dart into the bathrooms. No Denny. I glance outside at the rest of my class. Somewhat peaceful. Except I see Andy digging Scott in the ribs. That's a warning sign—I have to get back to the thirty-one soon. I rush back to our room—no Denny.

As I pass the kindergarten room, I see him emerge from the building blocks. He looks very much at home. As I stalk in and lead him from the classroom, I breathe a sigh of relief. He's safe.

Lord, a teacher will never question the parable of the lost sheep. She knows she has no choice but to leave the ninety-nine when one is lost, because she knows what might happen to the one lost and alone. Shepherds and teachers have that in common!

WHAT DO YOU THINK? IF A MAN OWNS A HUNDRED SHEEP, AND ONE OF THEM WANDERS AWAY, WILL HE NOT LEAVE THE NINETY-NINE ON THE HILLS AND GO TO LOOK FOR THE ONE THAT WANDERED OFF? AND IF HE fiNDS IT, I TELL YOU THE TRUTH, HE IS HAPPIER ABOUT THAT ONE SHEEP THAN ABOUT THE NINETY-NINE THAT DID NOT WANDER OFF (MATTHEW 18:12–13).

THE WRONG CLASSROOM

*H*ow's your class coming along?" I ask Shelly as we eat lunch together in her room.

"Well, they're not as good as last year's class," she begins tentatively.

"Mine either," I moan. "But they're beginning to understand classroom rules, so I guess that's a beginning." (My rules are simple: Don't talk without permission; Don't disturb others; Stay in your seat; Do your work.)

Shelly nods. "I think you have to be absolutely firm from the very first day. Otherwise, you'll never train children to be the best they can be."

"Or at least beginning the second day," I agree, remembering how much time I'd consumed the first day with Juan. But Shelly is right; the first day is best.

"If there are any secrets to good teaching," she explains, "I think they are good discipline, teacher commitment, and daily doses of praise to build self-esteem."

I nod in agreement. "How about half a papaya?"

Taking the papaya, she carefully peels the skin and cuts the fruit into slices.

I leave my half in the skin and spoon it out cantaloupe-style.

"Shelly, you are so methodical," I tease, as she consumes a tiny slice.

"But you're more creative."

"Maybe," I shrug. "But we're both terrific teachers." Teachers need heavy doses of self-esteem, too, even if they have to administer it to themselves!

As the bell rings, Shelly and I decide to show a film together that afternoon. We linger over conversation a minute to make plans. As a result of this last-minute decision my class precedes me into the room. Even before I enter I hear the bedlam.

Gary and Matt are having an eraser fight. Suzanne is standing on her chair, and everyone else is either talking or running around the room. I stand there a minute looking shocked, until I am certain they all see me. Then I turn and walk out the door, pretending to leave, but I stand just behind the door.

I hear the children whisper Shhh, and the sounds of desks creaking as the children sit down. In seconds it is perfectly quiet. I walk in again. They are sitting straight up in their chairs, hands folded, eyes riveted on me.

"You'll never believe what just happened to me," I begin with a huge sigh. "After lunch I walked into the wrong classroom. Children were running and fighting and yelling. It was unbelievable." I shake my head. "Believe me, I got out of there in a hurry! I don't know how I got so confused. It certainly is good to be back with you. I guess those children don't know classroom rules."

They exchange glances out of the corners of their eyes, unsure how to react. From now on I'll find them sitting at attention when I enter the room. Children's behavior rises to meet expectations. They would never want to be like the children in that other room.

Lord, what do you expect from me today? Help my behavior to rise to meet your expectations.

LOVE THE LORD YOUR GOD WITH ALL YOUR HEART
AND WITH ALL YOUR SOUL AND WITH ALL YOUR
MIND. . . . AND LOVE YOUR NEIGHBOR AS YOURSELF
(MATTHEW 22:37–39).

NO ROOM FOR DUCKS

When I began school this year I knew I'd have difficult children. Adams School always has more than its quota. But I never thought about ducks. This year I have a duck. His name is Dwayne.

Like Juan, Dwayne spent two years in kindergarten. Ever since the Disney channel became available in our area, Dwayne has been talking like Donald Duck. His parents have tried everything from speech therapy to intensive psychiatric care to help him, but so far no results.

The class has become used to Dwayne, but I have not. I feel as if I'm expected to teach a cartoon character, and I think that violates the terms of my contract. Having a talking duck in class is both unnerving and annoying.

Standing in line to come in from recess this hot afternoon, Dwayne is not only talking like a duck but making this awful quacking noise as well.

When I let the children leave the line one at a time to get a drink, Dwayne paddles off, even looking like a duck. Although I have read the psychiatrist's reports that describe Dwayne as an alienated child who needs my patience, I am suddenly left without any. The class senses my anger and becomes silent, except for Dwayne who continues his Donald Duck monologue.

I feel the explosion approaching, but I do nothing to try to control it, except to think momentarily that I should.

"Dwayne, that's it," I explode. "If you're going to stay in my class, you aren't going to talk that way. I want you to stop it right now," I add in my firmest tone.

The red-haired boy studies me intently, his face suddenly pale against a sea of freckles. Our eyes meet, locked together in combat. Finally his gaze lowers. I sense victory and send the rest of the class into the room.

"Make your decision, now, Dwayne," I state in my most severe tone.

"I'll talk the right way," he says slowly, but with great relief on his small face.

Donald Duck is gone, that easily, and I wonder if anyone ever thought to tell Dwayne not to talk that way.

After that episode, Dwayne settled down and became a better-than-average student. Being a duck apparently drained a lot of his energy. His parents were profusely grateful, and even the psychiatrist called to ask how I helped Dwayne through his problem.

Sometimes in education we become so involved in problems that we forget to try the simplest methods. "No" can be a valuable tool, but usually we only use it in anger, and then it's not as likely to be effective.

Lord, even my prayers for patience can be empty, nothing more than an echo of frustration. Thank you for helping me with Dwayne in spite of my own impatience. Even though impatience sometimes seems to work, teach me not to rely on it.

A MAN'S WISDOM GIVES HIM PATIENCE; IT IS TO HIS GLORY TO OVERLOOK AN OFFENSE (PROVERBS 19:11).

THE RIGHT ENVIRONMENT

*A*bsentmindedly I change the water in the vase that holds a rose Tammy brought me. Shelly, the other first-grade teacher, watches me with a grin of amusement.

"What's so funny?" I ask.

"I've just been wondering when you're going to realize that roses don't last a month," she smiles.

I survey the rose that I have been watering faithfully every day. It's as beautiful as the day Tammy brought it. I look closer and realize it is silk. I pull it out of the vase. The stem has mildewed.

Shelly begins to laugh. "Couldn't decide whether or not to let you water it all year." She smiles impishly. "It was a temptation."

"Hmm. It never occurred to me that it might not be real."

"Oh, well, look at it this way," she grins, tossing the mildewed rose into the wastebasket. "Not everyone can kill an artificial flower." The bell rings, and she suppresses a giggle and returns to her own room.

My class is lined up at the doorway, quietly awaiting me. It's been a couple of weeks since I walked into the "wrong" classroom, but they haven't forgotten it. I've never been able to tolerate a noisy classroom, even though some teachers claim noise is a productive, natural adjunct to learning. To me, noisy rooms feel wrong and chaotic. My own room has a buzz of conversation when we are doing art or some other kind of project. But that buzz has a different feel to it—it seems controlled and productive.

Lord, I like my classroom to be controlled and productive, but it occurs to me that my tolerance may be diminishing with age. People who kill artificial roses do not have all the answers. However, I'll continue to keep my own classroom quiet, largely, I admit, because it takes too much effort to regain control once it's lost. But help me not to be too critical of those who like their teaching environment a little less structured. After all, you taught some of your greatest lessons in less-than-perfect learning environments. Maybe we can all learn from one another.

JESUS WENT THROUGH ALL THE TOWNS AND VILLAGES, TEACHING IN THEIR SYNAGOGUES, PREACHING THE GOOD NEWS OF THE KINGDOM AND HEALING EVERY DISEASE AND SICKNESS. WHEN HE SAW THE CROWDS, HE HAD COMPASSION ON THEM, BECAUSE THEY WERE HARASSED AND HELPLESS, LIKE SHEEP WITHOUT A SHEPHERD (MATTHEW 9:35–36).

MARATHON MEETING

I don't like meetings of any kind, but Peggy, our principal, does. She has teachers' meetings every Tuesday after school. Consequently, every Tuesday I want to give up teaching altogether. Teachers' meetings held at the end of the day are the worst, because they can go on for hours. Peggy's always do.

After rounding up all the exhausted and frazzled teachers, Peggy announces, "There will be no more individualization of lunches among this faculty in the future."

"I don't understand what that means," Shelly says, echoing everyone's thoughts.

"You're one of the two people on this faculty most guilty of it. The other is Pat." She glares at me. "You two eat your lunch together in Shelly's room to the exclusion of the rest of the faculty. From now on you will all eat lunch together in Olivia's room."

I protest. "Anyone on the faculty who wants to join us is welcome. Besides, we've done it for years. Shelly and I are friends outside of school, and we talk a lot about our own kids and we plan things our classrooms can do together. After all, we're the only first-grade teachers."

"I certainly don't feel left out," Olivia adds. "I don't even take a lunch break, and I don't want anyone in my room at lunch because I use that time to tutor some of my children," she finishes firmly.

The rest of the faculty nods in agreement, except, of course, for Maggie, the third-grade teacher, who isn't here and who has not shown up at school yet this year. Though often late, Maggie is outdoing herself. It is already October and we've seen nothing of her.

Peggy continues, "Then it's settled. From now on everyone who does not have lunch duty will eat together in Olivia's room." Olivia winces, and Shelly and I exchange despairing glances. "And you will be happy about it," she finishes.

I will do it, but she can't make me be happy about it. We have so little free time that it seems we should be allowed to spend it as we please. I can think of no other profession that regulates even the lunch hour. And I can think of few ways more likely to make people *dislike* each other than to try to make them *like* each other. Besides, I'd lose valuable planning time as well as time to bounce problems and ideas off a trusted colleague. From the look on Shelly's face, I can tell she agrees. Olivia looks distressed at the thought of having her classroom become the center of social activity.

If Peggy notices our dismay, she does not acknowledge it. Instead she begins to read the calendar of school events. Her voice drones on, and the minutes crawl by. We all can read, and we all have our own copies. Why not let each of us read our own school calendar? I begin to feel like a child being kept after school for some unknown offense. Bone weary, I watch the clock approach 5:30. A meeting that should have taken fifteen minutes maximum has now dragged on for two and one-half hours. An army recruiter could enlist the entire faculty right now, I think to myself. We all would do nearly anything to escape. Perhaps Lebanon isn't so bad after all.

Suddenly I feel a giggle. Oh no, not now. When extremely

tired, I am given to uncontrolled bouts of giggling. Someone needs only to drop a faintly humorous line and I begin giggling like one of my own teenagers. Marty, the kindergarten teacher, provides the humor by asking, "Is this the school calendar?"

That did it. The giggles overcome my powers of restraint. Peggy stares at me sternly.

"Go get a drink, Pat," she commands.

Holding my breath until I reach Olivia's water fountain, I turn it on, forgetting for a moment that her fountain is the one that shoots water across the room. I realize one second too late that the spray is aimed at Peggy. As water pours down Peggy's face, Shelly reaches for paper towels and I try unsuccessfully to get the faucet unstuck. Olivia strides toward me, reaches under the sink for a hammer, and gives the knob a quick tap to stop the spray.

"I'm really sorry, Peggy." I try to apologize, but I am doubled over with laughter. I've been at school since 6:30 this morning, and fatigue has taken full control.

Shelly sits at the table, tears of laughter rolling down her face. Kate, the second-grade teacher, valiantly but unsuccessfully tries to control her giggles. Olivia, also chuckling, hides her head under the sink as though attempting to fix the offending faucet. Marty, the kindergarten teacher, gets up to go help Olivia, but she slips on the wet floor, falls forward, and lies sprawled face down on the tile, laughing so hard she can't get up.

Only Peggy remains stern and aloof. Saying not a word, she marches from the room, indignation resounding in every footfall.

What should have been a five-minute clean-up job takes us fifteen because we spend most of the time in unrestrained laughter.

In these unplanned, unprogrammable moments we find the togetherness Peggy demands of us.

Lord, help me to find a way to apologize to Peggy tomorrow and to be sincere about it. School administrators don't always have the easiest of jobs either.

FINALLY, ALL OF YOU, LIVE IN HARMONY WITH ONE ANOTHER; BE SYMPATHETIC, LOVE AS BROTHERS, BE COMPASSIONATE AND HUMBLE (1 PETER 3:8).

WORRY BEANS

*W*hile some of the children read with me, others work at their seats. But Angela, one of my better students, sits staring at the papers before her, her pencil resting beside them. I dismiss my reading group and stroll over to her desk. "Problem, Angie?" I probe. If she doesn't understand the assignment probably no one does.

"Not exactly," she flushes. Translated into first-grade language, that means, "I'm in deep trouble."

"How can I help?" I ask softly. "Which paper don't you understand?"

"It's not my work," she replies nervously as she studies her hand. "I was just praying."

"Something I can help with?" I ask, noting her taut little face.

"I was just praying that we don't have beans in the cafeteria at lunch today. I pray and pray every day. Because if we have them I have to eat them," she sighs.

Even though entire cold lunches may be thrown away, the cafeteria staff monitors hot lunches very closely. Every morsel of food must be consumed.

"Let me check the menu for you," I offer. In a minute I

return to Angie's desk with the good news. "It says spaghetti, Angie."

Her entire body heaves a sigh of relief. "I'll read the menu every morning first thing from now on," I assure her. "At least you'll know when the beans are coming. Maybe your mom would send a cold lunch that day if we let her know ahead of time."

She shakes her head. "She's a busy executive. She doesn't have time."

How can any mother be too busy to fix a cold lunch one day a month, I wonder. I jot a memo to myself to mention it at parent-teacher conferences. But I'll need to be tactful with the busy executive Angela calls Mom.

Lord, there are more prayers emanating from this room than my own. Help me to be more perceptive of the needs of these little ones. And Lord, is there anything at all you can do about the beans?

LET THE LITTLE CHILDREN COME TO ME, AND DO NOT HINDER THEM, FOR THE KINGDOM OF GOD BELONGS TO SUCH AS THESE (LUKE 18:16).

MAGGIE COMES TO SCHOOL

*T*oday is the first cool day of the school year, and it's Maggie's first day of school. She dismisses her substitute and seems surprised that we started school without her. Though somewhat frazzled looking, she seems to be the same old Maggie. Old, though, is a misnomer for Maggie. She is one of those people who will never be old. She admits being 62, but she has been admitting it for at least five years.

Maggie is dressed in her typical attire: red tights, a red mini skirt, a purple paisley vest, and a plaid fisherman's hat clinging tenaciously to the back of her head. I've never seen Maggie in anything but tennis shoes, and today is no exception. She always looks as if she fought her way out of a rummage bag. After getting to know her, people learn that she dresses this way because she is uninhibited enough to enjoy it, a true free spirit.

Maggie is the one person I think of when I read, "Blessed are the pure in heart," for there is no guile or deceit about her. Maggie's husband left her when their fourth child was born, and Maggie raised all four alone and gave them all college educations from her meager earnings as a teacher.

Maggie is not the best teacher I've ever known, but neither is she the worst. Discipline does not concern her, but her classes are no more rowdy than some in which the teacher *tries* to maintain control. In fact, it often seems that the children in her class form a protective cocoon around her. She inspires that kind of love.

But this year Maggie isn't her usual buoyant self. She seems drained and admits to being tired, something the old Maggie never would do. Privately, I think it may be because she climbed Mt. Whitney with one grandson, went windsurfing in Hawaii with another, took a two-week bike trip through the Appalachians with a granddaughter, and saw all the latest musicals and off-Broadway plays with her youngest daughter. But Maggie is convinced she is terminally ill.

She even met with Father Kramer, her Episcopal priest, and planned her last rites. In the tradition of her heritage, they will be Scottish. Scottish bagpipers will accompany the liturgy, and her class will do one last Highland Fling.

As she describes the extravaganza in minute detail during lunch, Shelly, always the realist, announces, "I can't take it anymore, Maggie. I'm making an appointment for you with Dr. Carlyle this afternoon. He is your doctor, right?"

"He'll just tell me the end is near," Maggie states.

"I don't believe it," Shelly scoffs. "Please do it—for all of us. We're a little tired of these ridiculous plans."

Maggie, crushed, turns to me for confirmation. "Is that true; you don't want to hear my funeral plans?"

"It's true, Maggie, because we don't think you're the type to die at a mere sixty-two."

Maggie trudges off. She stops making elaborate funeral plans, but she keeps to herself. And her illness remains a secret. Although we ask, she will speak to none of us about it. She spends lunches alone, ignoring Peggy's decree, and Peggy does not challenge her. Maggie does not show up when scheduled for lunch duty. We all cover for her, not knowing how else to help. We protect our own, even if we don't know from what.

Each time I see her I feel a stab of fear, and I pray, *We need Maggie, Lord. Do you need her more than we do?*

One day after the bell rings to announce the end of lunch, Shelly and I stop to talk a minute before going to our classrooms. Melinda, one of Maggie's students, rushes up to us breathlessly. "It's Mrs. McDonald," she yells. "She's on the floor."

Shelly and I exchange quick, panicky glances and race with Melinda to Maggie's room. Maggie lies stretched out on the floor, surrounded by thirty-four third-graders. "She's dead," someone shouts as Shelly and I push through the crowd.

"Everybody back," shouts Shelly.

We kneel on either side of Maggie. I feel for a pulse, and Shelly tries to hear a heartbeat. Suddenly, Maggie's eyes open and she yells, "Can't anyone take a nap around here without all this fuss?"

Rising quickly to her feet, she surveys Shelly and me. "Even if I was dead, don't you know you're not supposed to touch a dead person?" She turns to her class. "Enough of this nonsense! Everyone back in your seats. We were reading *Wind in the Willows*, were we not?"

Shelly and I creep out, not daring to look at one another.

Many months later we learn that Maggie had been slightly anemic, but otherwise as healthy and able as ever to meet adversity. And years later the whole incident still throws us into fits of hysterical laughter.

Lord, every school needs at least one Maggie to help the rest of us view the world from a different perspective. Maggie definitely adds sunshine and chuckles to Adams School! Thank you for letting us keep her with us. I know she will someday cheer all of heaven!

BLESSED ARE THE PURE IN HEART, FOR THEY WILL SEE GOD (MATTHEW 5:8).

MAGGIE'S CAR

*P*eggy knows how I feel about teachers' meetings. That's probably why she asked me to attend the one for the whole area. At least I will have Maggie to keep me company.

As soon as we are asked to attend, I make it clear to Maggie that we will travel in my car. As much as I dislike going to teachers' meetings, I dislike riding with Maggie even more. And although I like Maggie, her car is quite another matter. She has driven the same Morris Minor convertible for as many years as I've known her. I've been told that even when new it looked as if it had come from a salvage lot.

Besides its appearance, the top does not go up at all. Maggie maintains that the car dries out in the spring. No doubt it does, but that is little comfort when riding with her in a downpour. "The windshield wipers work," she always points out. But that seems a rather small advantage when the driver can't see the windshield.

Maggie's driving habits make riding with her risky even on a perfectly clear day. She is the only person I know who can pass between a tractor and a rig. She always drives 80 on the highways and 45 in town. "I've never had an accident," she boasts if someone begs her to slow down. "I have seen some really bad ones in my rear-view mirror, though," she'll add, oblivious to the fact that she probably caused them.

Unfortunately, all my careful planning for my safety did me no good. My own car, which has been terminally ill for some time, chooses the day of the teacher's meeting to belch forth huge columns of smoke. "That means something is really wrong, doesn't it?" I ask Jim anxiously.

He grins. "I don't think that's an overstatement."

Lord, Jim could never manage five children alone. Do you suppose you could cancel the teacher's meeting?

He doesn't, of course, so all day I teach my best—just in case I have to be remembered this way. At 3:30 I wait for Maggie to meet me in the office. At 3:45 I am still waiting. At four o'clock the office phone rings. "Are you there, Pat?" Maggie inquires.

"Of course I'm here. Where are you?"

"Well, I got out on highway 66 and was telling you all about my new reading program. You were being awfully quiet, even rude, I thought, because you didn't say anything. Then I looked over and the seat was empty. I'm about seven miles out of town. Do you want me to come back for you?"

"Well, I don't have time to walk seven miles," I retort.

I hang up the phone and walk to the front gate, arriving at the same time Maggie drives up. Honking wildly, she motions for me to join her. After the first near miss, I just keep my eyes closed.

Lord, you and many of your angels have kept watch over Maggie and her Morris for a long time now. All I need is a little assurance that today won't be an exception.

CAST ALL YOUR ANXIETY ON HIM BECAUSE HE CARES FOR YOU (1 PETER 5:7).

WHAT'S NEW?

*T*oday a professor from a local college is conducting an inservice meeting on reading. According to him, the latest and best method of teaching reading is whole language. His presentation makes a lot of sense to me, so I eagerly sign up for the class, even though it meets over the dinner hour, which means that chaos will reign at my house on Tuesdays. (More chaos, that is. There is always a certain level of it, which I am trying to learn to tolerate.)

The thing about the new reading method that bothers me, and it happens every time we find a new system in education, is that we are encouraged to throw out all that went before. Teaching phases ride high on the popularity charts, then suddenly, like last year's fashions, they are cast away. (And with them go thousands of dollars in textbooks and materials.)

Those of us who have taught a long time have seen the cycles come and go. "A child learns to read by sight," followed by "A child learns to read by phonics," followed by "A child learns to read by sight and phonics in combination, a linguistic approach." Now the "in" thing is whole language.

Shelly, Olivia, and I share coffee in Olivia's room after the meeting. "Every child is different, and each learns in a different way," Olivia offers. "For the best reading to occur we need phonics, sight, and perhaps this whole language, or any combination that works. There is no magic way for little ones to unscramble the system we call reading."

Shelly and I nod in agreement.

A teacher needs a very large bag of tricks to reach all the children in a class. I prefer to think that our bags are not yet full enough. I'm not willing to throw out anything that has worked. So I'll stuff this new method into the top of the bag and learn about it and try it out.

Lord, this is somewhat like religion. We keep arguing about which aspects of it are more important. Some emphasize your sovereignty; others emphasize man's free will. Some emphasize political action; others emphasize social action. As it is in teaching, I suspect it is in theology: we don't know it all yet. Your truth is more than we can comprehend this side of eternity. Keep reminding us that someone else might have part of the truth we have yet to discover.

AS THE HEAVENS ARE HIGHER THAN THE EARTH, SO ARE MY WAYS HIGHER THAN YOUR WAYS AND MY THOUGHTS THAN YOUR THOUGHTS (ISAIAH 55:9).

MORE THAN ONE
WAY TO HELP

*M*ichael's mother, a small-boned, very pregnant woman whose eyes dart nervously, stops by unexpectedly and says she just wants to see the room. "It's so bright and cheery," she observes.

I try to view it objectively. I have covered every available space with posters, projects, and student's work. She walks to the Super Star corner and finds some of Michael's printing. "He does really well, doesn't he?"

I nod. "I just moved him to the top reading group. It's like a light went on and the system suddenly makes sense to him."

"We've noticed that. He reads every sign up and down main street. Especially McDonald's. And he reads those little books you send home every night as if he's been reading forever. We really want him to be successful and happy in school before Heather puts in an appearance." She pats her stomach.

"It's a girl?" I ask.

"That's what the sonogram says. I know conferences aren't until December, but Heather is due around Thanksgiving and I just want to reassure myself about Michael's progress because I may not be able to make the conference."

"We could postpone it until Miss Heather approves," I suggest.

"I mean not be here at all." She suddenly starts to cry, and I help her to a chair. "I just have the worst nightmares about this baby. I think I'm going to die."

"Is there anything to indicate a problem?"

She shakes her head.

"Then maybe it's just last-minute jitters. With my kids, I always decided not to have the baby when I went into labor."

She smiles through her tears. "I've just been very lonely. My husband is a doctor, and I don't seem to fit this town's stereotype of a doctor's wife."

"Which is?" I prod.

"You have two kids, then you decorate a lavish house, and then you sit around being part of the decor of the local country club. I can't live like that." Large tears form again in her eyes as she finishes.

"Well, you can't die. Michael and Heather need a mother. Does your husband see you as a fixture at the country club?"

She shakes her head again. "He doesn't like it either, but his profession takes up so much time that it doesn't matter as much to him. We bought a house in this area because we saw some possibilities for historical preservation. So we're renovating it. That's acceptable," she adds sarcastically. "There are parts of this area of town that are all right to live in, but it's not all right to send your child to Adams School."

Suddenly I remember a young-looking doctor with stern but kindly eyes who visited my classroom last year, observing and asking all kinds of penetrating questions.

"I think I've met your husband. Did he visit last year?"

She nods. "We both know a school is more than a building. Everyone we talked with said this school has good teachers. They just couldn't understand why good teachers would stay in an area like this. But that was enough for us. If Michael could go to a good school in his own neighborhood, we were satisfied."

"But what about you?" I persist, knowing this visit has nothing to do with houses or neighborhoods. "Have you ever worked?"

"For ten years. I'm an RN, but I can't go back to work because we don't need the income and I really don't want to leave the children while they're young. But after ten years as a supervising nurse, it's hard to go cold turkey into vacuuming," she sighs.

An idea pops into my head. "What about something really part time, your own hours, and totally indecent pay, none, in fact, but it would use some of your professional skills?"

She looks interested.

"Our own school nurse from the district is here just one day a week," I explain. "But with the kind of children we have, it would be great to have someone come in more often. I'll have to check with the principal, of course, but I know she'll approve."

"I could even work before Heather is born," she offers eagerly.

"Should you?" I ask.

"I can't think why not. I worked with Michael until the pains were ten minutes apart. I think it makes labor easier."

I agree with her. The worst part of labor is when the hospital begins to take all possible precautions.

Her walk seems lighter as she leaves the room.

Lord, help me to remember that I can sometimes help the children best when I can help their parents.

THEREFORE ENCOURAGE ONE ANOTHER AND BUILD
EACH OTHER UP, JUST AS IN FACT YOU ARE DOING
(1 THESSALONIANS 5:11).

NITPICKING

I thought I was helping Carol, but, as it turns out, she comes to our rescue.

While everyone works alone, I stroll around the class, taking time to help children individually. As I do, I check each child's hair and ears. When I stop by Jose's desk, I notice activity in his long black hair. Lice time already, I think dismally. Wandering casually around the rest of the room, I see that Candy's long braids are also infested. Everyone else looks all right.

When we discover lice at Adams School, we call the parents and try to get them to treat the whole family, to wash the bedding, and to clean thoroughly. We try to explain that every school in our district has an outbreak now and then. But we know something else: when kids at wealthier schools get lice, their parents go into orbit and use every available method to get rid of them. At Adams School, lice are just part of the pattern of poverty, just one more thing to fight when there's no time or strength left. It does not mean that our parents love their children less; it means that sometimes fatigue and poverty win.

I search the cupboards in the school office, but our supply of lice shampoo has disappeared. Just then I remember our new school nurse. I call Carol and explain the situation, unsure what her reaction might be. To my relief, she bursts into laughter.

"I can get shampoo samples through my husband," she offers. "That should be enough, unless the epidemic gets too bad."

Jose's parents choose to shave his head. He won't be seen for a month without a cap. Candy's parents do nothing, so soon Tammy has it too. After dowsing two heads with lice shampoo, Carol and I spend several noon hours combing the nits out of each head of hair. Doctors assure us that nits just fall off, but teachers (and school nurses) know better. The nits that remain will often hatch another generation, even if only a few have missed the treatment. It takes a fine comb and infinite patience to pick the dead critters, one by one, out of hair.

Nitpicking is not one of the most pleasant ways to spend a lunch hour. I remember the first time I encountered head lice. My stomach churned, and my own head started itching violently. Jim had to search every inch of my scalp that night to assure me I had not been infected. Now, although there are at least several thousand things I'd rather do, I get a perverse kind of pleasure from capturing and combing out the nits that cling tenaciously to strands of hair.

Lord, a case of head lice is an unusual place to find a lesson in Christian living, but I think I see one. It seems to me that there is a great need for Christian nitpickers, people who patiently and lovingly help others remove the effects of sin from their lives. Too often we take the radical route of Jose's parents instead. In helping people get rid of sin's effects, we remove all traces of their dignity as well, leaving them ashamed and embarrassed. Then we wonder why we never see them again. Lord, is it sacrilegious to ask you to help me do more nitpicking and less headshaving?

LIVE IN PEACE WITH EACH OTHER. . . . WARN THOSE
WHO ARE IDLE, ENCOURAGE THE TIMID, HELP THE
WEAK, BE PATIENT WITH EVERYONE. MAKE SURE

THAT NOBODY PAYS BACK WRONG FOR WRONG, BUT
ALWAYS TRY TO BE KIND TO EACH OTHER AND TO
EVERYONE ELSE (1 THESSALONIANS 5:13–15).

A CHILD'S TRUST

*T*he idea seemed good at the time. The zoo from a nearby city offered to bring some of the smaller animals to visit each classroom. Since many of our children never get to visit a zoo, it would be an educational experience for them. But then I found out what the zoo considers a small animal. Small is not a word I use to describe boa constrictors.

The children and I watch in awe as the zoo volunteer describes the boa constrictor and its habitat while allowing the snake to wind itself around her neck. I shudder. I've always been terrified of snakes, even little ones.

"Now I'm going to let each of you pet Angelo," the volunteer announces. The girls in the class all gasp, and some of the boys' faces turn a little green. "And to prove there's nothing to fear, your teacher will go first."

Lord, is this absolutely necessary? Will these children be permanently damaged if their teacher refuses to touch a snake? I'll do it, but please don't let it get loose.

My heart begins to thump, my hands become clammy, and my shadow runs from the room screaming. But the teacher in me smiles reassuringly at the thirty-two faces intently watching me. I take a deep breath and reach toward the snake. The boa feels warm and dry; it is my own hands that feel cold and clammy.

One by one the children follow my example. If the teacher does it, apparently it must be safe. Good thing I'm not into jumping off cliffs!

After the boa, the owl and the ferret are calm stuff. At lunch time I scrub my hands as if I were about to perform surgery. Then I giggle as I wonder if the boa took a bath after being petted by all those humans with cold, clammy hands!

Lord, the children followed my example with barely even a thought about their own safety. Thank you for this reminder of how trusting and vulnerable children are. Please keep me from doing anything that would endanger them physically, psychologically, or spiritually.

NOT MANY OF YOU SHOULD PRESUME TO BE TEACHERS, MY BROTHERS, BECAUSE YOU KNOW THAT WE WHO TEACH WILL BE JUDGED MORE STRICTLY (JAMES 3:1).

ALL I NEED IS SLEEP

*A*lthough it remains hot during the day, nights are now cool. Autumn is upon us. The grapes have been dried in long rows of brown butcher paper and rolled like long rug runners into compact bundles. The cotton has been picked, and the fresh fruits of summer are gone. The brown foothills beg for mercy, thirsty from the long valley summer. In another month the rains will come, bringing relief to the hills.

Classrooms have been transformed by children's interpretations of pumpkins, witches, and ghosts. I wait to hear the comment I hear every year, which could have originated only at some teachers' college: "Halloween is the only real holiday for children." I don't believe it for a moment. Consequently, I am always the last to put up Halloween decorations and the first to take them down. I tell Mrs. Rodriguez, our room mother, "Just plan the party from two o'clock on." Then I try to put the whole thing out of my mind.

Peggy has different plans, however. She announces that we will start Halloween with a parade at eleven o'clock. Even Shelly, Kate, and Olivia, all Halloween enthusiasts, jump in with protests. "That's too much time to spend on Halloween." Since I think even an hour is too much, I nod vehemently.

Shelly adds, "If the children are in costume that early, we'll have total chaos by two o'clock." Maggie is not at the meeting to comment. She'll do whatever pleases her anyway.

"That's the way it will be," Peggy persists. "The parade will begin at eleven o'clock." She leaves no room for further argument, but it comes anyway.

"We can't afford to lose that much teaching time," I say, reiterating Shelly's and Olivia's argument.

"But Halloween is the only holiday for children," Marty argues.

"Then let them have the day off," I suggest.

Everyone stares at me blankly.

Finally, because it is 5:30 and we are all exhausted, we give in. We'll have Halloween this year, and we'll have it big.

Exhausted, I go home, only to discover that no one has started dinner. Five children and one husband are crowded around the TV, engrossed in Central America. "What's for dinner, Mom?" Kris asks as I enter.

I feel an explosion coming. I am tired, and I've worked longer hours than anyone in the family. The children aren't helpless; four are teenagers and know how to cook. That single comment, "What's for dinner?" must have driven saints to throw pans. It squeaks and grates on me like chalk on a chalkboard. Jim notes my mood and comes to my rescue. "I just got home myself, Pat and I didn't know what to fix. But go lie down. I'll find something for dinner."

I take him up on his offer. It has been a bad day, and I am suddenly exhausted and chilled. I turn up the thermostat and head for the bedroom. Once there, I toss my dress on a chair, pull off my shoes and pantyhose in one move, climb into bed, and turn the electric blanket up to nine.

It is dark when Jim awakens me. "I went out to get hamburgers," he explains, bringing me one on a tray.

"I have these kinds of days, too," he sighs.

70

I know he does. He's a social worker, and his day seldom ends at five. But I am still angry at four teenagers who do as little as they can. They make me feel as if I've failed as a parent, just as the children at school sometimes make me feel as if I've failed as a teacher. Tonight I won't work on records and plans until eleven. Instead I'll take a long, hot bath and climb wearily into bed. I'll definitely need the words of the Psalmist tonight.

Lord, help me remember that the difference between success and failure is often a good night's sleep.

FOR HE WILL COMMAND HIS ANGELS CONCERNING YOU TO GUARD YOU IN ALL YOUR WAYS (PSALM 91:11).

STALKED BY FAILURE

*M*orning does not bring refreshment. I am still tired and discouraged when I reach Adams School. As I correct the leftover stack of papers, I note how poor the children's work is. Even my top group did the assignment without the slightest indication that they knew what they were doing.

The autumn blues have attacked with vigor. Every teacher has moments when she wonders not only whether she's teaching anything, but whether students are actually losing what knowledge they had to begin with. If they lose a little knowledge each day, I might as well give up. Will there come a time when no one knows anything? What do I do when they reach zero? How can I be such a failure when I work so hard?

When the bell rings and the children line up to enter the building, I feel grumpy and ready to pounce. But the line is perfectly straight, and all I see are thirty-two angelic faces. Do they sense my mood or have they actually learned something?

I visualize myself before the school board justifying my teaching skills. "Yes, I know their SATs are worse than when they entered my room, but you should see how well they can line up." A giggle almost escapes, but I repress it. I am not in the mood for giggles.

I watch the children take their seats quietly. With their little hands folded, they await my words of wisdom.

Lord, I'm too weary to pray. Help me to better teach these little ones of yours. I feel failure stalking every step. These children are too precious for me to allow failure to win this battle. Please make me strong, and wise.

I begin to explain the day's written assignments to the groups. They listen attentively and immediately begin to work as I call the first reading group. Unexpectedly, memories of the chaos of the first week flash through my mind. I am suddenly rejuvenated. "Everyone gets a five-star bonus today," I announce as I dash around the room adding five stars to each child's card. At the end of the week, if they have enough stars, they get to take home a certificate embellished with stickers proclaiming them a "Super Star." I've always believed that positive discipline works better than negative. I prefer to reward that which is good rather than punish that which is not. I find I have to do very little punishing. "You're all just terrific," I add. They beam with delight and go to work with even greater resolve.

For a moment, or for a day or a week, I had forgotten that praise is its own reward (though stars and stickers help). I remind myself never to miss a moment to find something good in each child, no matter how slight or how fleeting the good behavior might be.

As the day proceeds, even the slowest readers do better than they have before. My feet are light. As I erase the chalkboard, the dust tickles my nose. I walk around the room, my domain, and watch the children work, stopping here and there to help a struggling child. I am at home and in love with teaching!

Thank you, Lord!

IN THE MORNING, O LORD, YOU HEAR MY VOICE; IN THE MORNING I LAY MY REQUESTS BEFORE YOU AND WAIT IN EXPECTATION (PSALM 5:3).

HALLOWEEN HASSLES

*H*alloween has come, just as I feared it would. I considered being ill this morning, but my conscience prevented that. So here I am, surrounded by a roomful of outer-space creatures, cartoon characters, clowns, and several others with layers of makeup.

After the pledge of allegiance, we line up for the big parade. I feel helpless at the total lack of structure. A space creature drops a play snake down the collar of a tiger, and the tiger screams with terror. The elephant, plumped with all of the family pillows, cannot sit down at all. The giraffe is two children who have assigned seats on opposite sides of the room. I give up on taking roll and mark everyone present.

Just as I begin to make some order out of all the chaos, Peggy appears with a sackful of candy for each creature. I try to stop her. "They don't need candy now," I protest.

"Of course they do," she insists. She passes out the candy, thoroughly amused by the children's antics. Fifteen minutes later, after Peggy has left, of course, they all have a sugar high. I try to remember why I didn't become an accountant. (Then I remember that I can't even balance a checkbook.)

I try leading a mob of first-graders to the school patio where the parade will begin. We fall in behind a mass of kindergarteners and begin marching around the patio, then around a six-block radius and back to the school. There the women of the PTA stand ready to give away prizes for the best costumes. Armed with note pads, they *ooh* and *aah* over the children. They reach no clear-cut decision, so we parade around again. The elephant steps on my toe. The giraffe has parted ways with itself, and the tail leads the mob; the head is lost somewhere in another class. The riot continues, and parents smile proudly as their children pass. "That's him," they announce, pointing out their child to nearby parents.

Suddenly I feel sorry for parents who spent hard-earned money buying a costume at the local discount store, thinking first of the child's pleasure and putting second the necessities that the money could have purchased. The child with a stay-at-home mom, who has both time and money to make a very special costume, will ultimately win. Other parents will purchase new costumes year after year, glowing with pride over children who will never win but will never quite understand why not.

Finally, Peggy mounts a box and bellows above the crowd of students, parents, and women of the PTA. "We have reached a decision."

Thank goodness. The blisters on my heels long for the first-aid kit in the room. Five huge stuffed bears are hauled out, and the children are suddenly silent with anticipation. But they won't go to a child who would remember it forever. Instead they'll go to a child who got one just like it last Christmas.

After the prizes have been given, we trudge back to the classrooms, where more sweets await the hyped-up children.

Was it a day just for children? I don't think so. I think a group of adults tried to recapture a vague memory of their own childhood, one which, in all likelihood, never existed.

By 4:30 I have restored the room to some semblance of order. In my box, I find a message from my oldest daughter: "I'm making dinner tonight." I smile at her thoughtfulness, grateful that one burden is lifted. As I drive home, through streets already streaming with creatures, I realize it is the poor who are out in force, those who do not yet heed the warnings that not all who pass out Halloween treats do it with kind intentions. It is a night for the less fortunate to glimpse the homes in better parts of town and to collect sacks of sugar that will cause cavities they can't afford to have fixed. Why would anyone say that Halloween is the only holiday for children?

Lord, help me to concentrate my efforts on giving the children what they need rather than what they want. Thank you for doing the same for me.

SEE THAT YOU DO NOT LOOK DOWN ON ONE OF THESE LITTLE ONES. FOR I TELL YOU THAT THEIR ANGELS IN HEAVEN ALWAYS SEE THE FACE OF MY FATHER IN HEAVEN (MATTHEW 18:10).

A REAL HOLIDAY

S ome teachers in poverty schools firmly advocate morning snacks; others believe it takes away valuable learning time. I cast my vote with the former. I've never thought my teaching abilities were outstanding enough to command attention over an empty stomach.

Even though many of our children's parents pick oranges for a living, oranges are a rare commodity in the diet of a migrant child or, for that matter, of any poor child. Charlie, down at the local processing plant, finds excuses to dump boxes of oranges regularly. I'm pleased that he chooses my car in which to dump them. The children rush for oranges with bright smiles and sparkling eyes. "Orange days" are great favorites for them. If children were to choose a holiday of their own, I suspect it would be orange day, raisin day, or even graham cracker day.

Maybe that's what makes a real holiday—sharing special moments with those we love. I don't think it has to be a day designated by calendars as a holiday at all.

Denny whispers in my ear, interrupting my reflections, "Are there seconds?" I study his hopeful little face and nod as I cut into another orange. "I love you, teacher," he says as he devours the orange. I'm convinced I am in the midst of a holiday for children.

Lord, may I never forget that I am teaching more than words and numbers. I am teaching skills and concepts that will help these children find a place for themselves in a world reluctant to give them one.

SUPPOSE A BROTHER OR SISTER IS WITHOUT CLOTHES AND DAILY FOOD. IF ONE OF YOU SAYS TO HIM, "GO, I WISH YOU WELL; KEEP WARM AND WELL FED," BUT DOES NOTHING ABOUT HIS PHYSICAL NEEDS, WHAT GOOD IS IT? (JAMES 2:15–16).

RAINY-DAY DESPAIR

*R*anchers have stopped watching the skies; their crops have
been gathered, stored, or shipped. Thirsty hills have
turned brown, impatiently awaiting seasonal rains. Time and
nature agree; rain is due.

But rain brings the worst of all worlds for teachers. It keeps
them indoors all day with thirty-two children who act like cattle in
a hurricane. It means no lunch break. In fact, it often means no
break at all. It means the best children will be at their worst, and
the worst will be beyond belief.

Teachers, like most other humans, recognize rain. My own
children recognized it from at least age two. They would press tiny
noses against the sliding-glass door and proclaim, "Wain, Mama,
wain." But with Peggy as our principal, the faculty of Adams School
no longer needs the ability to discern rainy days.

At the first sign of a cloud, Peggy adds to the front of her
office a large pole adorned with forty red and blue bandannas, the
kind used for the western look. Inside her window, she puts up a
sign that says, "And it rained forty days and forty nights."

"When the flags are flying, children do not go out to play,"
she decrees in her sternest voice. "Please check for the flags at all
times."

The whole effect boosts faculty morale so much that we

very nearly draw straws to determine who gets to be Noah. The thought of dear Noah spending all that time in an ark crammed with smelly, noisy animals reminds us of what we are in for during rainy season.

So when the rains come, we not only have to contend with the rain itself, but with Peggy's exasperating reminder that we are in for the worst of days. I sometimes dream of climbing the pole and ripping down the flags, one by one. But I am afraid of heights and intimidated by principals.

Lord, I know rain is a sign of your blessing. The earth needs it to produce the crops that sustain us. But when I am trapped inside my room with thirty-two restless youngsters, rain seems more like a curse. This year, whenever I am on the verge of giving in to rainy-day despair, remind me of next season's sweet, juicy oranges and the excited looks on children's faces on "orange days."

IF YOU FOLLOW MY DECREES AND ARE CAREFUL TO OBEY MY COMMANDS, I WILL SEND YOU RAIN IN ITS SEASON, AND THE GROUND WILL YIELD ITS CROPS AND THE TREES OF THE FIELD THEIR FRUIT (LEVITICUS 26:3–4).

COATS OF LOVE

*A*bout the time the first rains come, I also begin to notice which children do not have jackets or coats. Our rains are not like the gentle spring showers of the Midwest. They are unrelenting deluges of cold water. Coming down like heavy curtains, the rain can go on for days, sometimes unvarying, sometimes interspersed with bone-penetrating fog.

We begin the search for jackets by calling community aid services and the few parents with incomes above the poverty level. Some children will cling to the new jacket as if it's the best thing that ever happened. But more often, the jackets go home and are never seen again. Whether they are confiscated for another child, sold, or lost, I've never found out for certain.

Knowing that Juan, Javier, and Suzanne have been given jackets, I am troubled to see them cold and wet. "Where's your jacket?" I ask Javier. He simply shrugs and returns to building a tower of blocks the children enjoy on rainy days. Sometimes I wonder why I go to all the trouble in the first place.

But then I remember Jesus' words from Matthew 25:36: "I needed clothes and you clothed me." At Adams School, in spite of all our efforts, not all of God's children have coats. Before winter is over I will have lost count of how many jackets I've tried to replace. Whenever someone mentions an outgrown jacket, my eyes will light up and I will do whatever I can to see that the jacket ends up at Adams School. Sometimes whole wardrobes are contributed—those are the days when a teacher has a holiday just envisioning the happy smiles on the faces of the new owners.

Lord, thank you that I can express my love for you by meeting the needs of your children.

'WHEN DID WE SEE YOU A STRANGER AND INVITE YOU IN, OR NEEDING CLOTHES AND CLOTHE YOU? . . .' THE KING WILL REPLY, "I TELL YOU THE TRUTH, WHATEVER YOU DID FOR ONE OF THE LEAST OF THESE BROTHERS OF MINE, YOU DID FOR ME"
(MATTHEW 25:38, 40).

REWARDS

*M*rs. Fisher, how do you spell 'I got up late this morning and missed the school bus?' " I look at the grave face of the small, forlorn boy surveying me. Patches of his short black hair have been lost in a battle with blunt scissors. His shirt was new at least four siblings earlier. His shoes and shoestrings parted company long ago, causing him to walk with a scuff. Today the scuffing noise is accompanied by a sloshing sound, the result of his encounter with an irresistible puddle in front of our classroom. "So how do you?" he persists.

Most of the class is now able to write stories in their journals. They record their daily thoughts and feelings and, by doing so, learn about writing. But so far, Javier's journal consists of incomprehensible scribbling that even he cannot interpret. Yet here, in one small, rain-soaked little boy, is a teachable moment, a time when he's ready to learn.

"First, off with the shoes and socks, Javi," I command him, unable to ignore his sopping wet feet. "When they're dry, I'll put in some new shoestrings." All this comes before spelling, even though I'm concerned that Javier is in school so seldom. He and his eight siblings are sometimes in school, sometimes following the crops, and always struggling just to exist.

I put Javi's problems on hold while I stop the fight between

Jose and Suzanne. Jose, being remarkably tolerant, is letting blond, blue-eyed Suzanne pummel him with fierce blows. He turns to me helplessly, "I just came in the door and she attacked me."

I lead Suzanne to a small table and hand her clay, remembering that just last week she had come to school covered with bruises. I had called Child Protective Services, and Suzanne is now in a foster home. Her hostilities, however, are still very much in evidence. "You must be very angry," I comment gently as I hand her the clay. She grabs it from me and begins to mold small figures. Just as rapidly as she makes them, she massacres them. At least it isn't Jose.

Javi interrupts my thoughts as he tugs at my sleeve. "You didn't tell me how to spell 'I got up late this morning and missed the school bus.'" Now barefoot, Javier stands before me looking rather desolate.

"Let's sit down right here, Javi," I point to the bean bag chairs in the corner of the room. We take his sentence apart and talk about each word, not the whole sentence at once. Finished writing, he begins drawing puddles and a small boy jumping in them with obvious relish. I have a feeling that drying his shoes is a wasted effort. But in those moments working with Javier are glimpses of what teaching is all about.

Lord, my prayer list keeps getting longer and longer. As the year progresses, the underlying problems of these children become more and more apparent. Some days I find myself weary even before school begins. Thank you for the comfort of your Psalms. Please keep lots of angels guarding me and my little ones!

FOR HE WILL COMMAND HIS ANGELS CONCERNING YOU TO GUARD YOU IN ALL YOUR WAYS (PSALM 91:11).

A SUPER STAR FOR TEACHER

When the morning bell rings, the children go to their seats quietly, fold their hands, and wait for instructions, the super-star strategy again working effectively. In addition to the certificates sent home with children achieving super-star status, stars also entitle children to classroom privileges such as passing out papers and being line leader. Conversely, children lose stars for inappropriate behavior. Losing a star is a very serious offense. Whenever a student loses one, the rest of the class reassesses their own standings.

It works well. Johnny, never inclined to start any project he can postpone, announces, "I ain't workin' today." The rest of the class stops, eager to support the class dissident. I bend over Johnny's desk and whisper in his ear, "Just look how many super stars you have this week. You don't want to lose a star, do you?" Reluctantly, he takes his paper and begins working.

"What'd she say?" Matt whispers, glancing at me out of the corner of his eye.

Johnny pretends not to hear, a good response for an up-and-coming dissident.

"Red reading group," I announce. That means only ten children should be moving, but all thirty-two have to shuffle a bit. As the children gather around the reading table, I notice Matt has a new look. "Where did you get that football helmet, Matt?" He looks formidable encased in all that protection.

"My desk," he replies. I am always amazed at how much a first-grader's desk can hold. Schools would be wise to add wheels and rent them out as trailers during vacation periods.

"I'm not taking it off neither for nobody," he announces.

I have a very strong idea who nobody is. I consider what to do. Matt's mother had recently insisted that he was in the wrong reading group. Admitting that I may have somehow misjudged Matt's abilities, I agreed to try him in a higher group on a temporary basis. But Matt cannot keep up, and he knows it. Figuring that the helmet is his way of protecting himself from the embarrassment of being in the wrong reading group, I decide to let him keep it on. It's only a temporary solution. At lunch I'll make an appointment with his mother. Maybe together we can make the football helmet unnecessary.

At recess time, the children head eagerly for the playground, except those who have asked all morning when recess is. Now they are the ones asking if they have to go out. I nod. "But it's cold," they protest. (Why didn't they think about that earlier when they were asking about recess every five minutes?) In any case, they lose. The ten-cent cup of coffee in Olivia's room has more appeal than a roomful of first-graders in desperate need of a break to get the wiggles out.

The day goes on. Juan forgot his lunch. Liza threatens that her grandmother will beat me up because I allowed her to get her new coat dirty. It becomes a day like any other.

Why does any intelligent person teach, I ask myself as I wearily usher the last of the thirty-two out of the room. Then Liza comes dashing back in. She had forgotten her coat, the dirty one. On her way out she yells, "Bye, Mrs. Fisher. I love you."

That's what's so wonderful about teaching—children don't hold grudges, not even for dirty coats.

Lord, I feel like I've been given a super star, too. Help me to be as forgiving to others as my little ones are to me.

BEAR WITH EACH OTHER AND FORGIVE WHATEVER GRIEVANCES YOU MAY HAVE AGAINST ONE ANOTHER. FORGIVE AS THE LORD FORGAVE YOU (COLOSSIANS 3:13).

GOT 'EM IN MY HEAD

*M*ost teachers, myself included, teach math using manipulatives of various kinds. It makes math more real to the children. I usually use just plain beans, but more imaginative teachers spend hours transforming their beans into ghosties, froggies, turtles, and wee butterflies. Making all those little creatures wouldn't be my last choice of something to do, but it would rank pretty low. All of them, plain beans as well as ghosties, eventually end up on the floor, awaiting an encounter with the custodian.

When children can demonstrate that they understand addition and subtraction, we begin to memorize basic math facts. Wendy can do numbers to ten in a minute and forty-five seconds. Harry can do them in two hours and would take that long if I permitted it. Marta knows only how to subtract. She explains, "My mother only subtracts her checkbook. She's never added in her life."

"I don't need to memorize," Johnny comments. "I got 'em in my head," he advises his classmates.

They all look to me. "Keeping them in your head is just as good as memorizing," I agree. A math axiom by any other name serves just as well. It seems to be working for most of the children. Except Harry. He's up to three hours.

Lord, of all the things children need to keep in their heads, math facts are not the most important. In the few hours I have each day, help me teach things like love and faithfulness, which many of the children see little of at home.

MY SON, DO NOT FORGET MY TEACHING, BUT KEEP MY COMMANDS IN YOUR HEAḶṬ, FOR THEY WILL PROLONG YOUR LIFE MANY YEARS AND BRING YOU PROSPERITY. LET LOVE AND FAITHFULNESS NEVER LEAVE YOU; BIND THEM AROUND YOUR NECK, WRITE THEM ON THE TABLET OF YOUR HEART
(PROVERBS 3:1–3).

FOOD FOR THOUGHT

I'm so far behind in my planning that I've been coming to school early to try to catch up. It looks as if my plans will be thwarted this morning, though. Javi got here before I did.

"Why are you here so early?" I inquire, thinking of lost planning time.

"I got out of that house," he grins. "All the other kids were going to get a spanking. They have to catch me first." After pausing a moment, he asks, "Mrs. Fisher, do you think you got something for breakfast?"

"You're in luck, Javi. Remember that crate of oranges Simon's Produce gave us?"

He smiles.

Javi and I work out an agreement. I don't count the oranges he eats, and he doesn't interfere with my planning.

I try not to get too discouraged, but even with all my planning, progress in the lowest reading group is imperceptible. It's no wonder. Many of the children are from homes where education isn't very important. And many of the parents speak Spanish as their first language. They know enough English to get by, but not enough to help their children learn to read.

"Why wouldn't the farmer let the wolf in with the sheep?" I ask the reading group.

Jose smiles his most brilliant smile. "No sheep left, and one sick wolf from eating too much."

"Well said, Jose," I address my budding philosopher. Maybe there is hope after all. I'll hang on to that thought.

The top reading group reads everything, including my lesson plans. I encourage them every step of the way. They crave books, and it is their enthusiasm that often gives me the patience to work with those who have less.

Lord, thank you for Javier, oranges, first-grade philosophers, and gifted students. Give me enough patience and strength to reach them all.

AND LET US CONSIDER HOW WE MAY SPUR ONE
ANOTHER ON TOWARD LOVE AND GOOD DEEDS
(HEBREWS 10:24).

A BIRTHDAY FOR PATRICIA

*T*oday is Patricia's birthday. Pa-tree-cia, pronounced in soft Spanish tones. Patricia has been here from Mexico for two weeks. She knows only a few words in our strange language, and birthday is not one of them. But she does know it is a special day because everyone is "secretly" making her birthday cards.

Jose delivers the completed cards in a paper bag decorated with flowers, my contribution to the cause. Jose's lengthy speech is interrupted, fortunately, by a chorus of *Happy Birthday*. Lisa passes out the cupcakes her mother has made for Patricia. Mrs. Rodriguez, one of the mothers I depend upon most, explains her thoughtfulness. "I was afraid her mother wouldn't have time to make them after that long trip." I hug her because we both know Patricia's mother will never have either time or money for such frivolities as cupcakes and birthdays.

Patricia's eyes fill with happy tears, and she carefully stows the cards in the decorated bag. Weeks later I see her still toting around the tattered bag and cards. I offer to make her a new bag, but Patricia shyly shakes her head. This one holds the pleasant memories.

Lord, thank you for birthdays, surprises, and gifts of joy. Bless all the Mrs. Rodriguezes.

LET US NOT BECOME WEARY IN DOING GOOD, FOR
AT THE PROPER TIME WE WILL REAP A HARVEST IF
WE DO NOT GIVE UP (GALATIANS 6:9).

GUMDROP DRAGONS

I am amazed at how much these children like to write. They write in every spare moment, in addition to those I declare designated writing times.

"Wow, writing time, super!" Jason exclaims. "Did you ever have a class that wrote such good stories as we do?"

"Never," I assure him. It does seem that each year the children write just a little better than students from the year before.

I write for them, too—fanciful stories of villains, monsters, dragons, and marvelous first-grade heroes. Their favorite tale this year is about rescuing the kindergarten from a fearsome gumdrop dragon. It doesn't take first-graders long to launch an attack on gumdrops. Since I'm using some whole language techniques this year (such as lines that repeat), even Denny, Juan, and Jose can read them. The overwhelmingly favorite lines are: "We ate the green gumdrops, the red ones, and the black ones, too. We ate the purple gumdrops, the yellow ones, and even the blue. Then the dragon got smaller, and smaller, and smaller, you see. Soon he was smaller, yes, smaller, than me."

Sometimes I don't finish my story, and the children suggest conclusions. Often theirs are far more creative than mine would have been. Invariably, when my story is finished someone will ask, "Is it our turn now? Can we write stories too?" This is the moment I've been awaiting, and soon they are off and writing.

We like to publish our stories, too, like real writers. I type the pages of each writer's final draft, and the writer makes a cover out of cardboard and wallpaper. (That's what happens to those awful wallpaper designs that sell for ninety-nine cents in home improvement stores; they are snatched up by teachers in the publishing business.) After we assemble the book, the author illustrates it, and we have a new book for our classroom library, one that will be in great demand by other classmates.

One day I brought in a "real" author to talk with them, but I offended them deeply. "Aren't we real?" asked Michael.

Teachers learn something new every day!

Lord, you spoke in parables and all who heard stopped to listen and to learn. In some small measure, help my stories to do the same.

JESUS SPOKE ALL THESE THINGS TO THE CROWD IN PARABLES; HE DID NOT SAY ANYTHING TO THEM WITHOUT USING A PARABLE. . . . HIS DISCIPLES CAME TO HIM AND SAID, "EXPLAIN TO US THE PARABLE OF THE WEEDS IN THE FIELD" (MATTHEW 13:34, 36).

IT BELONGS TO JUAN NOW

*J*uan came to school today with his little body shaking from the cold. It is mid-winter, and he has on a tank top that is not quite long enough to cover his stomach and old corduroys with no remaining cord and a huge rip in one knee. On his feet are his father's shoes, at least nine sizes too large. He shuffles around the room trying to keep them from falling off while hitching up his pants in a valiant attempt to coerce them into a meeting with his shirt.

"Juan, do you want to find some new clothes from the clothes closet?" I ask.

He nods shyly.

Michael's old clothes have just been donated, and I remember seeing an especially nice sweater. At recess, Juan and I explore the closet. He finds Michael's sweater before I do, along with a pair of nearly new jeans, some brand new socks, and tennis shoes only a little the worse for wear. He also chooses an extra pair of jeans and a flannel shirt. We are out of winter jackets again, but together we find a sweatshirt jacket. When he joins the others after recess his eyes are sparkling and he's stopped shivering.

Just after we enter the room, Michael clings to me and whispers, "Juan has on my favorite sweater."

"I know, Michael," I reply, "but it was too small for you and

Juan had no sweater at all. Now that you can't wear the sweater any more, isn't it going to be fun to see someone else enjoy it? That's the only sweater Juan has."

Michael looks down at his gray fisherman's knit sweater. "I have plenty of sweaters, I guess," he admits grudgingly. "But it's not easy to share something you really want to keep."

"No, it isn't, Michael. I'll get it back for you if you want," I offer, not knowing how I'll ever be able to do it.

"No," he sighs softly. "It belongs to Juan now."

Lord, it's not easy to share the things we love. Michael is already learning what some adults never learn—that people are more important than things.

LIFE IS MORE THAN FOOD, AND THE BODY MORE THAN CLOTHES (LUKE 12:23).

THE TRANSFORMATION

*T*his may be the year we remember for record rains. We have just passed Thanksgiving—often the first week of the annual rains—and already the roof at Adams School is water-logged and leaking. I have hauled the plastic pails out of storage and placed them strategically around the room. The children have learned their way through the maze of brightly-colored buckets and seem oblivious to the idea that the situation might be unusual.

Chilled by the dampness, I turn up the thermostat, even though I know very well that it ceased working years ago, and pull my sweater closely around me. Most children are not as well protected with warm clothing as I am, but those who have jackets reach for them.

I note that Michael is not here. It's the first day he's been absent all year, and it's near Carol's due date. I remember meeting Carol the first time and think how she has changed from a terrified, wraithlike figure to a smiling, competent nurse. And she not only helped us conquer the lice epidemic, but she now keeps each child's health record updated and also takes care of all the classroom casualties.

Suddenly I am worried. *Take care of Carol, Lord*, I plead during a reading group. *Something within me knows that she needs your special care and love right now.*

The day drags on, and I find myself teaching on automatic. I've taught so long I can do it without much thought, and today my heart isn't in it. I glance at the clock. It is only ten o'clock. The rain still comes down in wind-swept sheets.

Even the children are quiet, unlike their ordinary, rainy-day unruliness. Perhaps I have trained them too well—I long for someone to challenge my authority. But no one does, and the hours crawl by. The reading groups come and go, and finally it is recess time.

I take the children to the bathrooms for a break from the classroom. Perhaps it will clear the cobwebs from our heads. They dash quickly across the unprotected stretch of sidewalk and back under the shelter of the eaves. Quietly they line up, and I begin my automatic count. Thirty-one. Yes, Michael is gone today, I am once again reminded. I shiver as I watch a car speed by and sweep waves of water in our direction. I gather the children around me as we enter the room.

The room has begun to smell like the waterlogged roof and thirty-one bodies. But despite the soggy, smelly conditions, the children are ready for math. They listen eagerly as I begin a review lesson, and they quickly provide the correct responses. I need not have taught that lesson, but review lessons are part of teaching on automatic. In desperation, I begin a math game. The children tolerate all this, but the feeling of oppressive stillness prevails.

I look forward to seeing Shelly at lunch, but I learn that she has offered to help Kate with cafeteria duty.

"Anything wrong, Pat?" Olivia asks, noting that I am playing with my food.

"Yes. My class is so well-behaved, they aren't even normal. Also, Michael is absent, and I can't get my mind off Carol."

"Why don't you call?" Olivia suggests. "Your class has caught your mood, Pat. Kids do that, you know. They sense that something is weighing on you."

I brave the rain and wind and fight my way to the office. I dial Carol's number, but the phone rings to an empty house. Another wave of panic rushes over me.

After the children troop in from lunch, I treat them to several stories. Then we practice songs for the Christmas program three weeks away.

Just as I am about to begin a writing lesson, the door bursts open and Michael and his father dash in. Each holds a bouquet of pink, helium-filled balloons proclaiming "It's a girl."

Michael grins his toothless grin as he distributes balloons to all of his classmates. Then his father brings in a cake decorated in pink and yellow. Suddenly the whole room takes on an air of festivity.

"When?" I ask Michael's father.

"Ten-thirty this morning," he grins proudly. "It went all right. Carol didn't have an easy time, but she's fine and so is the baby."

Relief spreads through me. "I'm so glad she's fine. I've been concerned all day. Is it still going to be Heather?" I ask.

He slaps his hand to his head. "I forgot," he mutters, dashing back into the rain. He returns with a bouquet of roses.

"For me?" I ask with surprise. He nods, and I read the accompanying note in Carol's familiar handwriting: *Can't wait until I'm in your first grade, Love, Heather Pat.*

I don't even attempt to stop the tears that roll down my cheeks and drip off my chin. No one notices them anyway. The children are stuffing cake into their mouths and playing with balloons. Nor does anyone notice the rain, the buckets, or the chill in the air. Happiness has broken through.

Lord, thank you for watching over Carol, and bless and keep little Heather Pat. Thank you for the miracle of this precious new life. Once again I am reminded that we too are children, your children, and that we are as dependent on you as this fragile newborn is on her parents.

MY GRACE IS SUFFICIENT FOR YOU, FOR MY POWER
IS MADE PERFECT IN WEAKNESS (2 CORINTHIANS 12:9).

TRYING TO UNDERSTAND

*A*fter the first few days of parent-teacher conferences, I am flying high emotionally, aglow with compliments from parents pleased with their child's progress. Eventually, I realize, however, that the parents of the brightest children sign up for the earliest conferences, eager to hear my words of praise and commendation about their children.

As I contemplate the upcoming conferences, which promise not to be so pleasant, Maggie's piercing voice interrupts my thoughts. "Some drunk on the phone for you, Pat," she pipes.

"What?" I ask, puzzled.

"There's some drunk on the phone in the office. Asked for you right away," she announces.

"You don't know who it is?" I quiz.

"Nope, I don't know any drunks," she adds, bouncing away.

Reluctantly, I cross to the school office. "Hello?" I say uncertainly as I pick up the receiver.

"Thish is Suzanne's mother," slurs the voice. "I had a con-con-con," she gropes for the correct word.

"A conference," I prompt, remembering that Suzanne had been returned home from Child Protective Services for a trial run.

"Yeah, one of those. Can't make it though—my hair's a wreck. You know when you set it and it just turns out bad? Anyway, jus' let me know how Suzanne is doing and I'll tan the hide out of her."

"We could schedule another conference," I suggest. Telephone conferences leave much to be desired. I like to be able to show parents samples of their child's work.

"Na, it's my hair you know—I need a perm or something." It was "or something," I was positive.

I think about Suzanne's report card—mediocre at best—and about her temper tantrums and her clay figures. She is a child emotionally wrecked. "Suzanne's doing as well as she can," I begin, realizing as I speak the truth in my words. Not well, I think, but surviving. Perhaps that is enough. And maybe, just maybe, I can find some extra moments to spend with her. Our part-time school psychologist might even be able to help, although the longer I teach the less faith I have in psychologists of any kind.

"S' good to talk with you," murmurs Suzanne's mother as she drops the receiver.

Shelly, who had been sorting her mail, looks up with amusement. "Well, was that a conference?"

"I have a feeling it's as close as I'm going to come."

"Getting one hundred percent of the parents here for conferences would solve some of the social problems of the parents," Shelly comments. "But I have enough difficulty just coping with the problems of the children."

I nod. The two are directly related. But Shelly is right—we can't do it all. I keep trying, though. Year after year I try to reach all of the parents, long after other faculty members have yelled uncle. But I am beginning to understand that some parents do as much as they possibly can by simply getting their children to school each day. Beyond that, the job of education belongs to us. Such trust and responsibility is both frightening and reassuring.

Lord, help me to be worthy of this trust, but keep me from being so consumed by it that I neglect other responsibilities. And protect Suzanne. Show her your love; she doesn't get much at home.

> YOU HEAR, O LORD, THE DESIRE OF THE AFFLICTED; YOU ENCOURAGE THEM, AND YOU LISTEN TO THEIR CRY, DEFENDING THE FATHERLESS AND THE OPPRESSED. . . . (PSALM 10:17–18).

WHAT WISE MEN!

*O*ur school is small, and so is our community, and in some ways we have remained untouched by rules governing larger districts. For instance, we can still celebrate Christmas for what it is—Christ's birthday. We can still sing "Away in a Manger" and "We Three Kings," although we are no longer allowed to re-create a full-scale nativity. But I remember with nostalgia my last three kings and their last visit.

At the end of a bone-chilling, rainy afternoon, I gave in to the beckoning of hot chocolate and a fireplace and left Adams School early. I had barely settled into my favorite chair when the doorbell rang.

Peering through the window, I saw three young teenage boys standing on the porch. Expecting another sales pitch for some cause like city basketball, I reached for my purse before going to the door.

When I opened it, three sets of eyes lit up with recognition and a trace of mischief. "David, Carl, and Joey!" I exclaimed in delight. "Come in!"

They hesitated briefly, glancing at one another, and then ambled into the house. They had been in first grade the first year I taught at Adams School.

David had been quiet at first, but after he learned to read nothing stopped him. When he reached junior high, I loved to see his name on the straight-A honor roll. Carl was the best artist I've ever had in class, gifted beyond measure. He and I had secretly agreed to find snatches of each day for his creativity. It was almost as if he would burst if he had to hold it in one moment longer. Yet his other work was always done well; that was his part of the agreement. I often wondered if I'd be able to afford one of his paintings when he became famous. I never doubted that he would be. Then there was Joey, whose mother and father had gotten a divorce when he was in first grade. For a while it seemed that no one would survive, especially Joey. Joey had been my favorite that year simply because he needed to be someone's favorite.

"We can just stay a minute," Carl mumbled. "We brought you Christmas presents." He blushed as he handed me a beautifully wrapped package, the wrapping paper a Carl original. In contrast, the packages from Joey and David appeared to have lost a tussle with a roll of scotch tape. I held their offerings on my lap in disbelief.

"Surely you guys have girlfriends to buy gifts for now," I protested. "I was grateful just to have all of you in class."

A flash of pain crossed Joey's face while Carl blushed and David flinched.

Noting their responses, I berated myself and changed the subject. "But how fun to be remembered. May I open them?"

They nodded with anticipation. Carefully I opened David's gift—a Christmas ornament labelled "World's Best Teacher—Mrs. Fisher." "David, what a nice compliment. Thank you. I love it. And there's a perfect place for it on our tree where everyone can see it."

"It's true—you were my best teacher."

"No way," interrupted Joey. "She was *my* best teacher."

"Mrs. Fisher, these guys are mere adolescents," Carl proclaimed. "You were *my* best teacher."

Tears threatened but I kept them back as I opened Joey's gift—six red, felt-tipped pens. "Oh, Joey," I laughed. "You remembered how I could never find my pen."

"Yeah, I always found it for you," he grinned.

"Well, I still can never find one," I admitted, "and every year I requisition another Joey to help me, but I've never been fortunate enough to get one."

He smiled.

I unwrapped Carl's package carefully, trying to save the original art work yet hoping the others wouldn't notice. The latest best-selling mystery paperback was inside. "Thanks, Carl, I've been wanting to read this."

"I remembered you always read mysteries," he mumbled.

"Really?" I asked with surprise.

"Why shouldn't I? Didn't you remember that I like to draw?"

Touché, teacher, I thought to myself.

"You boys have to have some hot chocolate before you brave that weather again," I admonished the trio.

"Sure," David agreed. The others nodded.

Over steaming cups of hot chocolate topped with marsh-mallows, we talked of the days that had been. "Are first-graders still playing the part of the wise men?" asked Joey.

"Not any more," I admitted. "But I don't know any year when I had better wise men than you three."

"I think we were just three wise guys," Joey replied.

"I remember when I dropped the gold. This kid from kindergarten tried to rip it off. Guess he thought it was real," laughed Carl.

After they left with packages of freshly-made fudge I had given them, I remembered that year, my first at Adams School. How fast they had grown. It all seemed less than moments ago.

I hummed as I began to prepare dinner. Every teacher needs to be someone's best teacher.

Lord, thank you for all wise men, but especially my favorite three.

WHEN THEY SAW THE STAR, THEY WERE OVERJOYED. ON COMING TO THE HOUSE, THEY SAW THE CHILD WITH HIS MOTHER MARY, AND THEY BOWED DOWN AND WORSHIPED HIM. THEN THEY OPENED THEIR TREASURES AND PRESENTED HIM WITH GIFTS OF GOLD AND OF INCENSE AND OF MYRRH (MATTHEW 2:10–11).

THE PERFECT PAGEANT

*T*his year my class can't sing. They simply can't. Other years we've learned the songs at least passably well. But this year, at each rehearsal for the Christmas pageant we seem to get a little worse.

Denny finally learned "Six Little Ducks," but that's the only song he knows, and he sings it no matter what the rest of the class sings. "And he led the others with a quack, quack, quack" is totally incompatible with "Away in a Manger." I've written myself a note in next year's plan book: *Do* not *teach* "*Six Little Ducks," ever.* Even though it's worked perfectly well for years, I'm unwilling to chance it again. I've tried to convince Denny to sing quietly; but the more I try, the louder he gets. It seems to be my year for ducks. At least Denny's infatuation has not revived Dwayne's interest in the subject. Dwayne has apparently renounced Donald Duck for good.

I try once again. "Denny, please don't sing 'Six Little Ducks' right now," I implore.

"But it's the only song I know," he protests.

"You can learn these others; I know you can. Please try."

He nods, but his eyes have that blank look again, and I know I've lost.

When we rehearse with the rest of the school, even Shelly, whom I can always count on for comfort and support, says casually,

"Your class was terrific last year—the best in the school. And there's always next year." Somehow I don't feel very encouraged.

I try to talk my husband out of attending this year's pageant.

"Jim, you don't have to go to the Christmas program this year," I offer. "There's a movie on television you've been wanting to see."

"Heavens, Pat, I wouldn't miss the performance for anything. Besides, for seven years I haven't been permitted to. Now, when there's going to be something unforgettable, you want me to stay home. Why I'd even consider *buying* a ticket this year," he finishes, his eyes twinkling like Christmas tree lights.

"When have I shown up at *your* last failure?" I taunt. "Never. Some people live by a code of ethics."

"Okay, Pat, if it means that much to you, I'll stay home," he sighs. "But I am in this marriage for better or for worse."

"It won't be just 'for worse,' Jim. It will be bad beyond belief."

"Then I definitely need to be there."

And he is. So are parents, aunts, uncles, cousins, neighbors, physicians, farm laborers, attorneys, fruit packers, the unemployed, the poor, and those that mourn. I am in the latter category.

At the last moment before leaving for the program, I change into my bright red dress.

"I thought you hated that dress," Jim comments, looking surprised.

"I do," I reply. "But I don't have anything else that is red, and when I blush from embarrassment I want to be able to say it's the reflection from my dress."

But I had forgotten something very important: When it's your child performing, nothing can go wrong. As the final chorus ends with a piano crescendo, Denny's unmistakable voice sings, very loudly and very alone, the grand finale, "And he led the others with a quack, quack, quack."

To my amazement, a thunderous ovation breaks forth.

Carol comes up to me, her eyes glowing with delight. "It was just darling," she smiles.

I search her face for traces of sarcasm, but I detect none. Heather Pat, wide-eyed from all the excitement, stares with all the wisdom of a six-week-old from her mound of blankets. There is hope for the future, I think, touching her soft cheek with what I hope is reassurance.

On the way home, Jim says, "I can't believe you would have let me miss that, Pat. It's an experience I'll never, never forget." He then laughs until tears roll down his cheeks. Soon I join him. Sitting in Baskin-Robbins, I begin my recovery with a huge banana split, complete with a maraschino cherry and double whipped cream.

Later, when I am in bed and Jim is snoring softly beside me, I begin to think. The Lord sent his Son to us as a little baby. He probably would have loved "Six Little Ducks."

Lord, thank you for Denny and his six little ducks and for joyful noises and for putting all these things into perspective.

SHOUT FOR JOY TO THE LORD, ALL THE EARTH,
BURST INTO JUBILANT SONG WITH MUSIC (PSALM 98:4).

TIME FOR THE OTHER FIVE

I never want to stuff another bear as long as I live," comments Kris, my eldest daughter, as she surveys the room filled with thirty-two bears.

"Me either," I agree. "Next year we'll do kittens."

She frowns. "That's not exactly what I meant. No more stuffed animals ever."

I was afraid that's what she meant. Hopefully she'll forget by next year.

"Right now I have to get these wrapped," I begin.

"And I have homework to do," she explains, leaving the room.

"I'll help, Mom," offers Amanda, my youngest. "I can do it."

So I settle for the help I can get and wonder, as most mothers must, why children stop helping the moment they can be of real assistance.

Every year it seems more and more difficult to assemble thirty-two Christmas gifts. But every year I have a Patricia, a Juan, and a Denny, and I know that my gift might be the only one they receive.

I smile as Amanda wads tissue paper around a bear and reaches for a piece of yarn, struggling with teeth and fingers to convert it to a bow. I reach for my seven-year-old and give her a hug.

She grins. "What's that for?"

"It's for being you," I smile, realizing how grateful I am for my own children, including the one who just deserted me for calculus and terminally bad music.

Lord, sometimes I get so involved with the thirty-two children at school that I don't give enough attention to the five at home. It's not easy to work and be a mother, too. Help me to keep my priorities balanced.

Eventually we finish our makeshift wrapping. Amanda and I take a hot chocolate break, and I take time to listen to Amanda's thoughts about the world.

ABOVE ALL, LOVE EACH OTHER DEEPLY, BECAUSE
LOVE COVERS OVER A MULTITUDE OF SINS
(1 PETER 4:8).

IS THERE A PRESENT FOR ME?

*R*ain pelts the roof as I stare forlornly at the brightly-colored packages. Kris and Amanda troop into the living room, Amanda still struggling with her shirt buttons. "Use larger garbage bags for the bears," Kris suggests. "I'll help," she offers. "But first you need to check out the French toast Trish is making in the kitchen. She's trying to boil it."

I think Trish may have inherited my cooking talents, but even I never thought of boiling French toast. Jamie and Megan are sloshing down bowls of cereal as I enter the kitchen. "We were going to have French toast," Jamie sighs, "until we saw who was making it."

Deciding that being a mother takes priority over getting to school early, I begin turning out French toast by the loaf. Still stuffing mouthfuls, the five help me wrestle packages into the car. "Thanks, Mom, for the great breakfast," yells Jamie as I pull out of the driveway. His comments make the delay worth every second. I decide to work out a better solution to our family's breakfast dilemma.

Once at Adams School, I debate whether I can carry three garbage bags at once through the driving rain. Just then Butch, our custodian, darts out to the car. Butch is like a little boy at Christmas, hoping no one forgets his gifts. He spends most of the last day before Christmas vacation going from one room to another in search of gifts. This year I bought him a large box of his favorite candy.

"Saw you drive up with all that stuff, Pat. Let me help," he offers as he opens the car door and starts hauling garbage bags.

The two people most needed in a school are the custodian and the secretary. I smile as I remember the wise advice of an education professor in college. "Be sure to get to know the custodian and the secretary at your school. They're the people who run the place." Liz, our school secretary, only works part time because of the size of our school, but she always does a full-time job in the four hours she works. For her, I bought stationery to write to her son stationed in Germany who won't be home for the holidays.

With Butch's assistance, I arrange the thirty-two packages under the tree, knowing that thirty-two sets of eyes will be unable to stray from them all day.

Denny approaches my desk first. "Is there a present under that tree for me? I haven't been good all the time," he confesses.

That had to be the understatement of the year. But as I look at Denny's quivering little mouth, I think how much we adults misinterpret Christmas to children. After all, we got the best gift ever at Christmas—God's Son—and it certainly wasn't for being good. It's downright destructive, as well as theologically incorrect, to teach children they have to deserve Christmas.

"Of course there's one for you, Denny," I answer, hugging him to me.

His eyes sparkle. "My mom said no Christmas this year because we don't have any money, but I'm having Christmas right here!"

I make a note to check with Emergency Aid to see that

Denny's family's name is on the list to receive a Christmas basket. I think his name was on the list I sent in last week, but I want to be certain.

Soon I gather all the children around me. We sing Christmas songs, and I read the Christmas story. Finally I give in and pass out packages. As Denny clutches his bear in one hand and a candy cane in the other, he smiles with pure delight. "It's all free; I didn't even have to earn it."

"That's what Christmas is all about, Denny," I assure him.

As I watch the children prepare to leave for Christmas vacation, their eyes alight with anticipation and happiness, I too, feel happy and content.

Lord, these gifts we share today, not just the bears, but the love and happiness, are but a small reminder of the gift beyond measure, the real gift of Christmas, the ultimate gift, a tiny baby, your Son, a gift that changed the world for all time.

As I clean the room, I listen to Handel's *Messiah*. My mind drifts to Christmases past—when I held my own little babies on Christmas Eves. Now the French-toast eaters await me at home, having rattled every gift under our tree. "Oh Come, Oh Come, Emmanuel," I hum as I lock the door to my room, watch Shelly do the same, and wave a "Merry Christmas." Tomorrow Shelly and I will meet at the best little restaurant in town for lunch—our Christmas gift to each other every year—good friends sharing special time, special talk, and special happiness. But today we are both tired and anxious to get home.

TODAY IN THE TOWN OF DAVID A SAVIOR HAS BEEN BORN TO YOU; HE IS CHRIST THE LORD. THIS WILL BE A SIGN TO YOU: YOU WILL FIND A BABY WRAPPED IN CLOTHS AND LYING IN A MANGER (LUKE 2:11–12).

A CHRISTMAS GIFT

*A*s Shelly and I enter The Valley Oak for an early lunch, we note with delight the festive Christmas decor. In the Old Oak room a huge Christmas tree, adorned with ornaments from around the world, twinkles with tiny colored lights. On each table are fresh, fragrant greens and large red candles. We sniff the combination of greens and delicious food.

"Let's see how they decorated the Golden Oak dining room," Shelly urges. "It's smaller and a better place for conversation." The doorway is framed in greenery sprinkled with artificial snow and garnished with huge red velvet bows. Inside, warmth and light from a blazing fire radiate through the room, and bevelled windows sprayed with artificial snow add to the cozy atmosphere. "Here," Shelly suggests, as she chooses a table near the fireplace.

"Look at the stockings hung by the fireplace. They must be for each person who works here," Shelly comments. "Most adults probably like the Old Oak room better. The decor is more sophisticated in there. But I like it here better. Probably because I'm something of a kid myself," she grins. "Teachers have to be, don't you think?"

Nodding in agreement, I comment, "I think all teachers cling to moments of childhood."

We place our order for Cajun blackened red snapper, our usual choice, and settle down for serious conversation.

First we catch up on families. Shelly's two daughters will be home for Christmas next week from the small college they attend. I fill her in on Christmas plans for the seven in my family.

When the waitress serves our lunch, we enjoy the tasty food in a few moments of silence. But soon our deep friendship pulls us back into earnest conversation. The waitress refills our coffee cups and asks if we would like dessert. We decide against having any; good conversation is a better complement to any meal than the best chef's richest dessert.

We reminisce about the first half of the school year, then discuss teaching plans, future projects, and general teaching philosophies. Eventually we get to all the things that are wrong with education and our ideas for correcting them.

The waitress continues to refill our cups, but it's the conversation we have come for. We discuss each of our children in detail, politics, and how we would solve world crises.

I realize time is passing, but these are the conversations Peggy forbade us to have, half a year's worth. Catching up takes time.

Finally, when I begin to feel as if I have taught a whole day, I ask Shelly what time it is.

She looks at her watch. "Four-thirty," she grins sheepishly.

"Well, it takes a while to solve all the teaching problems we have plus the problems of the rest of the world," I rationalize.

As we prepare to leave, the waitress jokes, "I was beginning to wonder if I should bring you a dinner menu."

Shelly and I have set a new record for ourselves: a five-hour lunch.

Jim bursts out laughing when I get home from lunch just as he's arriving for dinner. "I believe it," he teases. "No one can talk as much as two teachers."

Lord, thank you for good friends and understanding husbands. And thank you for the Child who brings out the youngster in all of us at Christmas.

I TELL YOU THE TRUTH, ANYONE WHO WILL NOT RECEIVE THE KINGDOM OF GOD LIKE A LITTLE CHILD WILL NEVER ENTER IT (LUKE 18:17).

THOUGHTS ON A FOGGY DAY

*T*he joys of Christmas—lighting the Christmas candle of the advent wreath, wrapping last-minute gifts, worshiping at midnight services, and enjoying family—pass too quickly into the doldrums of January, the bleakest of all months.

Starched sheets of heavy fog layer the Valley, filling every crevice, and extending to every corner. From my position on the playground, fog totally obscures Adams School from view. I pull my jacket closely around me, and my mittened hands search deeply into my pockets for warmth.

I hear on the way to school that the airport is socked in by fog and that police are requesting everyone except emergency traffic to stay off the roads.

Despite the warnings, Peggy and the rest of the district refuse to call off school for fog. The only concession to its potential danger is to sometimes delay school for two hours, supposedly giving the fog time to lift. But today it hasn't lifted an inch.

Bone-chilled, I consult my watch. I've been outside only ten minutes. I shiver involuntarily and force myself to walk around what I assume is the general vicinity of the playground. Most children have sought refuge in their own classrooms, which open early on days like this. My own students huddle in the doorway, waiting for me to finish supervising children who aren't here and whom I couldn't see if they were.

Even on pleasant days, playground duty leaves me feeling forsaken. Being surrounded by swarms of people half my size is a very lonely experience. But being alone on a foggy playground is eerie as well as lonely. If I get lost out here today, I wonder if anyone will come to look for me. Probably not. "Pat," they'll say, "she used to teach here but she got lost in the fog one day. We haven't seen a trace of her since." It is not a comforting thought.

I look at my watch once again. Only fifteen minutes have elapsed. Time stops on a playground. I long for an adult to talk with. I long to be at home. (Except if I were home, I would be sick; and if I were sick, I would have had to rewrite all my lesson plans so that a substitute could decipher them. Being sick is not worth the effort.)

But I promise myself that some foggy day I will stay home. I'll curl up in my robe and slippers in a big chair, read a long-awaited mystery, and drink cinnamon-spiced tea. I know, of course, that I'll never *really* do it; I would wonder the whole time what was happening at school! But thinking about it makes the cold more bearable and the time pass more quickly.

Lord, thank you for pleasant thoughts that overcome moments of despair and loneliness.

THE MIND OF SINFUL MAN IS DEATH, BUT THE MIND CONTROLLED BY THE SPIRIT IS LIFE AND PEACE (ROMANS 8:6).

THE MYSTERY OF MISSING FLAGS

*R*ain is falling, but the bandanna flags are not waving under the eaves in front of the office. Peggy's sign is also gone. As I check my mailbox before school, Peggy stomps from her office, obviously in a grim mood. "Do you know anything about our rainy-day flags, Pat?" she demands. "They're missing."

"No. I haven't seen them since yesterday."

"No one has," she pouts, stomping back into her office.

On my way to my own room, I stop at Shelly's. She looks up quickly from the stack of papers she's correcting. "I didn't do it, Pat, honest," Shelly maintains, intercepting my unasked question. "I would have loved to, but I never would have had the nerve."

Another rainy day followed, and in place of the bandanna flags flew a single red flag. On it with black marker had been written the single word: *Rain.*

The mystery of the missing bandannas was never completely solved. But one day in the spring, long after the rains had stopped, Maggie showed up in a bandanna patchwork skirt, embroidered with "It rained forty days and forty nights." While we all eyed her skeptically, she explained, "When my oldest daughter heard the story she loved it so much she made this skirt and sent it to me." No one could ever be sure her story wasn't true, even Peggy.

The day the bandanna flags disappeared we had all been dulled by nonstop rain, and we needed a reminder that a day would come when it wouldn't rain at recess. I still suspect we have Maggie to thank.

Lord, thank you for all your promises, especially rainbows.

NEVER AGAIN WILL THE WATERS BECOME A FLOOD TO DESTROY ALL LIFE. WHENEVER THE RAINBOW APPEARS IN THE CLOUDS, I WILL SEE IT AND REMEMBER THE EVERLASTING COVENANT BETWEEN GOD AND ALL LIVING CREATURES OF EVERY KIND ON THE EARTH (GENESIS 9:15–16).

THERE GOES MARY POPPINS

*A*ngela received an umbrella from her executive mother and proudly shows it to the class at share time. It seems a practical gift for an independent youngster who walks to school in all kinds of weather.

It is not raining today, but the playground is covered with huge puddles from previous rains. The lunch recess aides instruct the children to stay on the blacktop, but there are 350 children and only two aides, so they have trouble enforcing their order. One of the children is bright, creative, and slightly-mischievous Angela, who manages to get her umbrella outside without being stopped by anyone.

"I'm Mary Poppins," Angela begins boasting.

Apparently not getting the response she wants from the other children, she declares again, "See, I'm Mary Poppins." This time she sweeps across the blacktop onto the treacherously muddy playground.

"Look, Angela is Mary Poppins," Michelle yells. "She's going to fly."

That is all it takes. What first-grader can refuse a noontime flight over the school?

"C'mon," yells Angela, her umbrella held high over her head as she races across puddles to gain momentum. Behind her, my other thirty-one first-graders follow at full speed to view her takeoff.

Angela is not Mary Poppins, and neither is anyone else. Not everyone lands in the puddles. But fourteen of them, all mine, emerge with mud from ears to toes.

Liz has to locate fourteen parents. The lucky ones only have to bring clean clothing. The less fortunate ones have to take a mud-laden child home for a bath.

"You are *not* Mary Poppins," Angela's mother tells her through clenched teeth. "Do you hear me? And you will never have another umbrella before you are thirty years old."

I expect Peggy to be angry. But instead I find her and Liz laughing heartily after the last of the mud kids has left.

"You have a bright one there, Pat," she grins, shaking her head. "Is she always so creative?"

I nod in agreement. "I think she's a definite candidate for the gifted program though I'm going to wait for SAT scores to recommend her. Her work is outstanding. She's creative and a good thinker. But she's not Mary Poppins."

Peggy and Liz laughingly agree.

Never again will mud puddles be the same for me. I will always think of Angela and Mary Poppins.

Lord, thank you that Angela wasn't Mary Poppins. I need her right here! But is there anything you can do about mud puddles?

LET THE CHILDREN COME TO ME, AND DO NOT HINDER THEM, FOR THE KINGDOM OF GOD BELONGS TO SUCH AS THESE (MARK 10:14).

FREE FROM TIME

*T*his morning has been terrific. Everything is flowing so smoothly that we even have extra time for each reading group.

Matt seems overjoyed at being able to keep up. He's a marvelous little boy, and his mother now seems able to appreciate him for what he is—a jumble of freckles, bright red hair, and deep dimples—and accept that he is not the best reader in the class.

And Javier is slowly, haltingly starting to read. Though needing continual reassurance, he is learning. His bus is always late, so we have a few moments after school to read together. Javi sinks into one bean bag chair and I collapse next to him in another.

Juan, too, is starting to read. "These are real words in a real book," he assures me, at the same time looking for reassurance. He's come a long way from the little boy who wouldn't get off the floor.

"Absolutely right," I smile at him. "Just look at the way you are reading them!" He beams. I know he still has a very long way to go, but beginnings are important.

We finish math early, too. Most of the children have given up using beans in favor of using their fingers to figure problems. They're not quite into memorization yet. Some know addition and subtraction beyond ten, and Jason is already up to carrying and borrowing.

We even have time to write this morning. Terrific stories continue to emerge from these vivid imaginations. The spelling isn't always correct, and the handwriting leaves a bit to be desired, but the ideas are wonderful!

I'm as excited as my students when we begin to write. I write along with them, continuing the adventures of a wonderful first-grade class. They have no difficulty identifying with these heroic boys and girls.

With no warning, Shelly barges in, interrupting my educational fiesta. "Isn't your class coming to lunch, Pat?" she asks.

I look at her curiously. "It's only 10:30," I protest.

She steps in and stares at my clock. "Your clock stopped, Pat. It's 11:45, and your class is the only one not in the cafeteria."

We hurriedly pack our books and rush to line up, lunch pails clanging.

For a long time I'll remember the day the clock stopped and what a joy it was to have extra time.

Lord, maybe I need to begin to live more for the glorious moments of teaching and to be less time conscious. But as Ecclesiastes tells us, "Everything in its time," and now it's lunch time. You know the importance of that. Hungry people do not learn well. You performed a miracle with five loaves and two fish so that five thousand of your followers wouldn't have to go hungry. The only miracle I can do is open thermoses (sometimes)!

THERE IS A TIME FOR EVERYTHING, AND A SEASON FOR EVERY ACTIVITY UNDER HEAVEN (ECCLESIASTES 3:1).

EMERGENCY

*T*he alarm clock rings, and I instinctively glance out of my bedroom window to check the weather. Fog again, thick curtains of it. It's lingering later than usual this year. I slip from bed and turn on the radio. "The following school districts are reporting foggy day schedules," the newscaster announces. Near the end of the long list I finally hear "Kent City—Plan C." That means school won't start until 10:30, and the buses won't run until 10. Plenty of time for a leisurely breakfast of bacon, French toast, juice, and coffee.

When breakfast is ready, we sit down for a relaxed, though not quiet, meal. Each time the foggy day schedule is announced again, the children cheer. "Maybe they'll cancel school altogether," Jamie mutters hopefully.

"They'll never do that," Kris replies as she spears another piece of French toast.

"Kent City has just gone to Plan B," the announcer breaks in. That means the fog is still too thick to risk putting buses on the road but that school will start at 10:30 for those who don't depend on bus transportation. It also means that parents have discretionary authority to keep their children home all day.

"Wish we rode the bus," Jamie sighs, knowing he'll never

benefit from discretionary authority because we live only two blocks from his school.

I remember to wear my warmest clothes. No doubt Adams School will have little or no heat. Butch, who controls the heat, not only drives a school bus but lives far out in the country. We'll be lucky to see him at all today.

As I get into the car, I note that the fog has grown even more dense. I inch along, suddenly grateful that my old car finally succumbed to its terminal disease and that I am now driving an almost new one. Unable to see through the fog, I stop where I know there are traffic lights. Then I guess whether they are red or green. The radio further discourages me. "There's a nine-car pileup on Route 66. Do not drive, we repeat, do not drive, unless it's an absolute emergency." It would indeed be an emergency if I were to leave the twenty-four youngsters who do not ride the bus without a teacher.

Suddenly my thoughts are interrupted as the car ahead of me pulls into the intersection and into the path of a car traveling at an unreasonable speed. As the two cars collide, I see a man thrown brutally from his car, his body arching above the trees. I pull over quickly and rush to the scene. The speeding car stops only momentarily, then continues on with another burst of speed. Running to the fallen man, I expect to find a dead body. Instead I find him moaning in fierce, unrelenting pain. Bleeding from mouth, nose, and an almost severed ear, his knees twisted akimbo, he mutters, "Gotta get up."

"No, you must lie still. An ambulance is on the way," I assure him, wishing it were true.

A woman runs out of a nearby house. "What can I do?" she yells.

"Get some towels and blankets and call 911," I yell back.

I try to hold the man down as he attempts to struggle to his feet. He's small, perhaps five-feet, eight-inches, 140 pounds or so, but his injuries seem to have given him superhuman strength. When the woman returns with the blanket and towels, I beg her to stay and help.

"I'm sorry," she says, "but I'll get sick. But I did call 911," she assures me before returning to her house.

Lord, it's you and me now. Mostly you. I press the towel on the ear and the cut that descends to his neck and at the same time try to hold down the rest of his body.

After what seems like ages, I hear the wail of an ambulance. *Please, Lord, hurry.*

"The ambulance will be here any minute," I reassure the man. "You're going to be all right." *He will be, won't he, Lord?* I begin praying the Lord's Prayer aloud. It seems to comfort him, so I repeat it again and again.

Finally the ambulance arrives and the professionals take over. A policeman takes my name and address and looks at me quizzically when I say, "I'm a teacher; I have to get to school."

I drive the last few blocks to school at a snail's pace and pull in just as the first bell rings. As I enter the office to check the bulletin, Shelly yells, "Pat, Pat, what's wrong? You're bleeding!"

I look at my clothes and realize that the man's blood has drenched me.

"There was an accident. But I wasn't in it," I explain hastily. "Shelly, could you get that extra outfit from my closet?" I always keep extra clothes at school. I learned long ago that clothes do not always survive first-grade art projects. It's always an outfit I can't bear to see in my closet, yet can't justify giving away.

By the time Shelly returns with the clothes, shock has hit me and I am shaking uncontrollably. Peggy pours me a cup of steaming coffee.

"Drink," she orders.

I obey, and the warmth swirls through my body.

"Can you teach today?" Peggy asks.

"I'm all right," I answer a little more firmly. "No more coffee, though." I hold my hand over the cup so she can't add any.

Some parents kept their children home even though they don't ride buses. So I have only fifteen children. We read, write stories, and do the kind of art projects a teacher is afraid to attempt with thirty-two students. But all day I keep thinking of the man who had been so severely injured.

The accident made me realize that playground duty prepares teachers for a multitude of unexpected things. If there's blood, we run toward it. It goes with being a teacher.

Lord, this time I got through it because you were very near. Thank you for your presence in all my times of need. Watch over your servant, Lord, I don't even know his name.

EVEN THOUGH I WALK THROUGH THE VALLEY OF THE SHADOW OF DEATH, I WILL FEAR NO EVIL, FOR YOU ARE WITH ME; YOUR ROD AND YOUR STAFF, THEY COMFORT ME (PSALM 23:4).

GRATITUDE

*T*oday I receive a call from Don, the man who had the accident. He still has a lot of pain and says it will be a long time before he walks again.

"I want to thank you," he says. "If you had let me get up I probably would have died, they tell me."

"It was hard," I admit. "It's good you aren't very big or I wouldn't have been able to hold you down."

"I'm six-feet, two-inches and weigh 190. What do you consider large?"

No wonder I had so much difficulty. The shock of the accident must have caused that much mental distortion. And I thought I was being so calm and objective!

"I want to repay you," he says. "Not that I can ever do enough, but I'd like to do something—send you flowers, a gift certificate for dinner-for-two, or something."

"No, I could never permit that," I answer firmly. "You can repay me by helping someone else sometime."

Later I learn that Don has returned to work, and still later I see his picture in the paper along with that of an attractive young woman to whom he has just become engaged.

Lord, could you imagine the good Samaritan accepting a free dinner or receiving *flowers*? As for *rewards*, I'll take mine in heaven. I'll need them. After all, I'm a teacher!

FOR WHERE YOUR TREASURE IS, THERE YOUR HEART WILL BE ALSO (LUKE 12:34).

FIRST LOVE

I want to read a really thick book," Jason announces as he hands me a copy of Tolstoy's *War and Peace*.

"Does your mother know you brought this one?" I ask.

"Not quite," he answers softly, his eyes lowered. In first-grade language, "not quite" means "definitely not."

"All right, Jason, you can read it if you can read the first page."

He can't, of course.

"You know, Jason, thick or thin doesn't count when it comes to books. We all like to read for fun, and that's the kind of reading you should be doing. I've got some special books for super readers tucked away in this drawer." I fight to open my crammed desk drawer.

"Harder than the first-grade ones in the bookcase?" he asks hopefully.

I nod as I pull out a *Ramona* book, one I haven't read to the class yet. His eyes light up when he determines it is indeed for older children but that he can read it.

For weeks I watch him devour *Ramona* books, often at times when he is supposed to be doing something else. I ignore some of these instances because a small boy has fallen in love with reading, and that's what my job is all about. First loves of all kinds are important. Each time Jason returns a *Ramona* book for a new one, he and I share a moment of joy, a small secret—we both love to read.

"I get butterflies in my stomach sometimes when I see a book I want to read," I confide in him.

He smiles with understanding. "It makes me think of pizza with pepperoni and black olives."

Lord, thank you for children like Jason and the special joy they bring. Let this one always love Ramona and reading.

CAST YOUR BREAD UPON THE WATERS, FOR AFTER
MANY DAYS YOU WILL FIND IT AGAIN
(ECCLESIASTES 11:1).

HOME TO STAY

*T*oday the class gets to visit the school library and hear the librarian read a special story. Then each child will choose a book to take back to the classroom to read. I have always enjoyed library time, but this year we have it at 8:30, during my reading time, and nothing can interrupt reading and remain in much favor with me.

The children choose their books and trudge to the reading circle. I look for Denny, but then remember that he is absent today. The librarian has chosen a story about the adventures of some animals, and each child gets to play the part of one of the animals. They are eager and enthusiastic, and we stay until I see Kate's class lined up outside awaiting our departure.

Quickly I line up my class, and we begin our trek back to the classroom.

As we approach the room, I hear loud sobs. I stop the class, put a finger on my lips for total silence, and look around.

Jason points excitedly. "Over there, behind the bush. It's Denny."

Sure enough, Denny is huddled behind a bush, sobbing as if his heart were breaking. "Denny," I call, the dew-drenched bushes slapping my face as I reach for him. "Come on out."

He comes, hurtling himself at me and hugging my hips. "I

thought you were gone," he sobs. "I came to school late and the room was empty."

"We'd never leave you, Denny," I assure him. "We were just in the library. Remember, today is library day? I thought you were absent; that's why we didn't wait for you. Now see why I get so frightened when I lose you?" I hug him to me. "I'll make a deal with you, Denny. You don't ever wander away again and we won't either."

He sniffles his agreement.

Lord, maybe my little lost sheep is home to stay.

THEN HE CALLS HIS FRIENDS AND NEIGHBORS TOGETHER AND SAYS, "REJOICE WITH ME; I HAVE FOUND MY LOST SHEEP" (LUKE 15:6).

LEARNING TO LOVE

S pring has finally come to our valley. Buds on the trees are swelling, eager to burst forth to greet the warming sun. A few brave daffodils paint lavish yellow images against green spring lawns. Even the rain seems even-tempered and gentle.

Now that my class has learned to make heart shapes, we spend every spare moment composing valentines. So on art day, when Suzanne asks, "Can't we make valentines again?" I am at first exasperated. But then I remember how her fists used to pound everyone in the class and how she used to devastate clay figures. Now she wants to make messages of love. I give in, and we make valentines again.

Surveying my desk after school, I realize that most of the valentines are for me. I chuckle at Denny's "Luv u tehr." Most of them say "You're a great teacher." Though young, they've learned to say the right words. But it is Suzanne's valentines that stop me. There are several, rather neatly cut for Suzanne, but all they say is "I."

"Suzanne, you didn't finish your valentines," I remind her the next day.

"That's 'cause I don't love nothing," she replies defensively.

147

Oh, Lord, I thought we were beyond that. It hurts to think Suzanne still has found nothing to love.

Later that day I hear Suzanne's voice. "Mrs. Fisher, look. Come here *fast!*" I rush to our science corner to see our butterfly emerging from its cocoon. "Look, just look," she points excitedly. Soon there are thirty-one other pairs of eyes watching in hushed expectancy as the butterfly frees itself for a first fling around the jar.

"What will we do with it now?" Suzanne asks breathlessly.

"What should we do?" I ask her.

"Take it out to the oak tree and turn it loose," she announces.

Balancing the butterfly jar, Suzanne leads the rest of us in a procession to the oak tree. Once there, she carefully unscrews the lid. The butterfly lingers for a moment on the rim of the jar, then it dips its wings in a final salute and disappears into the distance.

That afternoon Suzanne comes up with another valentine. "I want to write 'I love butterflies,' but I need help with the spelling."

We spell the words together, and she returns to her desk and begins to draw a brilliantly-colored butterfly.

Lord, please help Suzanne find someone to love. And help me to show her yours.

IF I SPEAK IN THE TONGUES OF MEN AND OF ANGELS, BUT HAVE NOT LOVE, I AM ONLY A RESOUNDING GONG OR A CLANGING CYMBAL (1 CORINTHIANS 13:1).

SERVANT OF THE LORD

What would I do without Mrs. Rodriguez? Not only has she been room mother all year, but she comes in three mornings a week "to give a little extra attention to those not doing so well." Lisa, her youngest, certainly does not need extra attention; she's been at the top of the class since the first day. Mrs. Rodriguez comes for those like Denny, Juan, Jose, Suzanne, and Patricia.

"How do you manage with seven children, working all night cleaning those offices, and then coming to school to help?" I asked her once.

"Things are easy now," she smiled in reply. "John and Laura are at the University on full scholarships, and Mary has graduated and has her own classroom in L.A. So I just have four at home. But those first days after my husband was killed—they were hard, let me tell you. There I was with seven children and only a sixth-grade education. But I was determined not to be on welfare. It wouldn't be good for the children, you see," she explained. "So, it was just me and the Lord, mostly the Lord."

She'd done it, too. With her own hands and with the assistance of the older children, she had even built a new home.

Her first name is Maria. but no one calls her that; she's

Mrs. Rodriguez to everyone, and indeed she has earned that respect.

When she arrives she immediately goes to work with the lowest group, pulling them out one by one and reading with them as I've taught her to do. She points to each word and reads along with the child, setting a pace at a speed the child can read. Words read in this manner reinforce the child's reading skills and are more likely to be remembered. The time she spends with each child is time I will never have, and each time her neat, trim figure enters my room I am again grateful for a special woman named Mrs. Rodriguez.

Now that I'm using more whole language activities as an adjunct to teaching reading, Mrs. Rodriguez makes big books out of some of our favorite stories. She prints and illustrates the stories on posterboard-size paper. Then, as I hold them up to the class and point to the words, the class chants the stories. Even Denny, Juan, and Suzanne know these stories because we do them again and again. It's an excellent supplement to reading and a place where some of my lower students can achieve success.

"I think I can learn to read," Juan said the other day. And he said it with such confidence that he convinced me too!

Self-esteem is such an important ingredient in the learning process that any time an extra dose can be given, it's definitely worth the effort. This year I have Mrs. Rodriguez to thank for much of this extra help.

Lord, thank you for your special servant, Mrs. Rodriguez and the example she is to all of us.

SHE SPEAKS WITH WISDOM, AND FAITHFUL INSTRUCTION IS ON HER TONGUE (PROVERBS 31:26).

MISPLACED MASTERPIECE

*M*ost principals do a supervised visit during reading or math, but I can tell more about the quality of teaching if I visit during unstructured times like art," Peggy announces.

I know immediately I am in trouble.

We are painting today—big green shamrocks and whimsical leprechauns—then adding coins we have cut from leftover metallic gold Christmas wrapping paper.

I try prevention. I cover the floor and all the desks with newspapers. I am as well-prepared as I possibly could be, I think.

When Peggy appears for her visit in a white silk dress with berry shoes and accessories, panic rises within me. I long for an extra newspaper with which to drape her.

As she strolls around the room, I keep my eyes on Juan, Denny, and Suzanne, the most likely candidates to usher in disaster.

Denny, his tongue tucked in the corner of his mouth, proceeds with great care and small amounts of paint. Juan carefully outlines his picture first with a pencil. Even Suzanne seems cautiously absorbed. I breathe a sigh of relief as Peggy proceeds from student to student exclaiming enthusiastically.

Then she stops at Wendy's desk. A top student, always neatly dressed, Wendy has a quiet, unassuming manner. She has never caused me a moment's concern all year. She is every teacher's dream child. Until that moment.

Without warning, over goes Wendy's paint, splashing erratic shapes on Peggy's dress. Then over goes the bottle of glue, followed by the gold coins. The students gasp in unison, then fall into total silence.

I rush to Peggy. "Let me help," I cry, though I have no idea what I can do to help.

"You've done quite enough, Pat," she says, eyeing me sternly. "This was my very best outfit. Notice I said *was*." She stalks from the room.

Both Shelly and Olivia laugh when I tell them.

"But it didn't happen in your classroom," I agonize.

"It was her fault, Pat," Shelly maintains. "Everyone in education knows how unpredictable art projects can be, especially in primary grades."

Olivia tries to encourage me. "When I saw her coming from your room, the effect of green and gold against the berry and white was striking!"

Striking or not, my evaluation this year will say something about being unprepared in art. Next year I'll bring a clear plastic raincoat for visitors.

The next morning I enter the office as quietly as possible to check my mailbox, hoping to avoid Peggy. But as soon as she sees me, she comes out of her office.

"Pat, I'd like to apologize for what happened in your room yesterday. It was obviously not your fault. When I finally got over the grief of my dress, I realized it was my fault for coming to a first-grade art project dressed in that manner. If it's all right with you, I think I'll observe a reading lesson for your yearly evaluation."

Lord, thank you. That is absolutely fine with me.

THERE ARE DIFFERENT KINDS OF GIFTS, BUT THE SAME SPIRIT. THERE ARE DIFFERENT KINDS OF SERVICE, BUT THE SAME LORD. THERE ARE DIFFERENT KINDS OF WORKING, BUT THE SAME GOD WORKS ALL OF THEM IN ALL MEN

(1 CORINTHIANS 12:4–6).

ARE THERE "ENNYMORE"?

*S*umming up my accomplishments with Denny this year makes a rather brief list: He now knows his whole name and can write it; he doesn't get lost in class or even on the school grounds; he can read a little; and by working frenetically with beans, he can sometimes do a few math problems. Shelly, Olivia, Maggie, Peggy, and George, our sometimes psychologist, are of the same opinion: Denny will benefit from another year in first grade.

"I guess I'll have Denny again next year," I sigh at lunch one day.

"Is Shelly going to have Kenny, then?" Marty, the kindergarten teacher, asks curiously.

When deciding about Denny, we had not consulted Marty. After all, we weren't thinking about returning him to her.

"Kenny?" we ask in unison.

"Denny's little brother," she explains. "You know, the little boy who always gets lost—the one with blank eyes. Other than the eyes, he doesn't look much like Denny, though."

"Maybe he ought to stay in kindergarten another year if he's anything like Denny," Shelly suggests.

"That won't work," Marty replies. "Benny, the younger brother, enters kindergarten next year. And Renni, the little sister, begins the year after that."

We all stare at Marty in amazement. "You've met with the parents?" I question. "They didn't show for my conference."

Marty nods. "They showed. They were just an hour late, and you had left. They got lost on the way," she explains. "They love the teachers their children have, so Pat and I get them all by parental request."

Shelly has the nerve to laugh. Kate, the second-grade teacher, looks depressed. She realizes she is next in line.

So Denny would go on to Kate, and I'd have Kenny next year. And then Benny and Renni.

Lord, I'll have to spend the next few years in an in-depth study of the parable of the lost sheep. And I'll certainly need Psalm 91.

Olivia places her hand on my shoulder. "Look at it this way, Pat. There's Denny, Kenny, Benny, and Renni, and then we're through."

"Unless there are 'ennymore'," quips Shelly.

I glare at her. Sometimes even best friends can strain the limits of friendship.

Lord, I know I've done my best with Denny, but it hasn't been enough. Grant Kate the wisdom to help him where I have not.

MAY THE FAVOR OF THE LORD OUR GOD REST UPON US; ESTABLISH THE WORK OF OUR HANDS FOR US— YES, ESTABLISH THE WORK OF OUR HANDS
(PSALM 90:17).

FIRE!

*T*he warmth of coming summer is in the air today for the first time this year, and Peggy has gone to an all-day administrator's meeting.

"It's too nice to spend a lunch hour in a stuffy classroom. Let's move a table out to the school patio and have a picnic," Kate suggests.

Soon we are all basking in warm sunshine and casual conversation, but our peaceful moments are suddenly interrupted by Marty. "There's smoke coming out of Maggie's room!" she shouts.

"Nonsense," Maggie snorts, but she too turns to look.

"That's honest-to-goodness real smoke," yells Marty as she takes off running toward the room.

The rest of us follow as though competing in a sixty-yard dash. We yank open the door to Maggie's room, then stand in stunned silence as we assess the situation. Maggie had left her teapot on a hot plate and it had boiled dry, burning through the teapot and feeding the flame with nearby papers.

"Everybody grab something," Maggie yells as she doles out more pots and pans than I have in my whole kitchen at home.

Most of the water we throw is intended for the fire, but we aren't a baseball team so our aim leaves something to be desired.

Nonetheless, within five minutes the fire is out, leaving a sodden, burnt-smelling mess in Maggie's room.

"This kind of thing happened in another school where I taught," Kate confides. "After the fire, teachers were never permitted to cook anything in their classrooms again."

Although cooking is certainly not an integral part of the curriculum, most of us make popcorn for Friday afternoon treats. And Marty's class sometimes makes cookies or does some other kind of cooking project.

Olivia sums up our feelings. "We have few enough privileges. I, for one, don't want us to lose any more, even though I seldom cook in my room."

We surveyed Maggie's blackened wall with corporate gloom. Finally Marty said, "Well, Peggy isn't here today. I have rolls and rolls of wallpaper that I use for art projects."

"If we all come in right after school we could scrub the wall, clean up this sodden mess of papers, and then paper the wall," I suggest.

"I'm sure this is just surface damage," Shelly adds. "And by tomorrow it will be dry. So no one will ever know."

"I'm for it," Olivia agrees, and the others nod their assent.

Everyone is on time for this teacher's meeting, including Maggie. We lug out papers damaged either by the fire or by the amateur firepersons. Then we scrub the blackened wall until only dark smudges remain. Finally we roll out long pieces of wallpaper, grateful that it is the self-adhesive type.

Even though we waste a lot of time giggling and untangling Maggie, who always seems to be between the wallpaper and the wall, we manage to finish by five o'clock.

"It looks bright and cheerful. Changes the whole room," comments Shelly.

"Anybody hungry?" Olivia queries.

"Starved," moans Kate.

"Good, the pizzas will be here any minute," Olivia grins. "My treat."

Over huge slices of pizza, we admire our work.

At the next faculty meeting, none of us dares to look at each other when Peggy says, "Stop by Maggie's room sometime. Some of the rest of you could use some of the creativity she has."

Lord, thank you that our faculty can find togetherness in important moments and that we're not too busy to take care of each other when it counts. Help us to continue to protect Maggie, and also protect us from her good intentions!

CARRY EACH OTHER'S BURDENS, AND IN THIS WAY
YOU WILL FULFILL THE LAW OF CHRIST (GALATIANS 6:2).

TESTING THE TEACHERS

*T*he time has come again for SATs, yearly tests that are intended to objectively measure progress students have made. What the tests really measure are a few areas in each subject that someone we don't even know has deemed important. My classes score well on the test because I emphasize basics. But no test measures creativity, the ability to think, or the sum of a child's learning. Test results are like a snapshot; they freeze one moment in time. Though not by design, SATs also reveal how few things can be measured objectively.

Some principals demand a certain percentage of improvement on test scores each year. This encourages teachers to "teach for the test" because classes vary so much. "Give them a bit of practice in how to fill in the bubbles," Peggy advises. "That way the test format won't intimidate them. Then depend upon the fact that you have taught well all year. The test will be a measure of some of the things you've taught. It's like a synopsis; it doesn't tell the whole story."

Nonetheless, I am exasperated on the day of the test when I get a new little girl. Coming to us from a school and a teacher that did not consider the basics important, Sonja is well below even the bottom of the class. Her score will undoubtedly bring my class average down. Since in our community the SAT is considered a test of teaching ability, her performance will affect my rating. I don't mind being tested on the students I've taught, but I do mind being held accountable for someone I didn't even teach.

Shelly, too, is upset. She lost one of her best students just before the test. Now some other teacher will reap the rewards of Shelly's efforts.

But in spite of its limitations, the SAT is important because it demands some accountability from teachers. After all, we deal with a very precious commodity: children. And the future of our country depends upon the excellence of its teachers.

Lord, help me to concentrate my efforts on things that are important to the children and be less concerned about how their performance will affect people's perceptions of me.

EACH OF YOU SHOULD LOOK NOT ONLY TO YOUR OWN INTERESTS, BUT ALSO TO THE INTERESTS OF OTHERS (PHILIPPIANS 2:4).

THERE WAS A RAZOR ...

*A*ngela, escorted by her indignant mother, arrives at school early this morning. "I had to bring her to show you," the mother exclaims. "I didn't know what else to do."

Looking something like an outer-space creature, Angela stands before me with huge tears glistening in her eyes. Her eyebrows are totally missing.

"What happened to the eyebrows, Angela?" I ask softly.

"I . . . I shaved them off," she sobs.

"Why?" I inquire.

"Because there was a razor and my eyebrows," she cries. "I didn't know it would look so bad."

"Do you have any eyebrow pencil?" I ask her mother.

"Sure," she says as she hunts through her purse.

Angela's new eyebrows aren't perfect; they are just a lot better than they had been. After peering at herself in her mother's compact mirror, Angela heaves a huge sigh of relief and heads for the playground.

"What am I going to do with her?" her mother moans.

"Well, you'll have to continue with the eyebrow pencil until they grow in."

"No, I realize that. What am I going to do with Angela? First Mary Poppins, now this; and it's only first grade."

"Be really, really grateful for her," I reply.

She looks startled.

"Angela does those things because she's very creative. She's bright and gifted. I just got back her SATs, and she only missed one on the whole test. That's ninety-ninth percentile."

"But that's not the way gifted kids were when I was in school. They were always the most well-behaved; they sat with their hands folded and did everything the teacher said."

"Angela does mind in the classroom, but she's not perfect the way you describe gifted children. I suspect that the children you remember were what we now call 'greenhouse gifted.' They're bright students but very conforming. It's the Angelas of the world who make the great writers and scientists. They're the truly gifted people in any field," I finish.

"Are you telling me this is probably just the beginning of her 'experiments'?" she sighs. But at least she is smiling.

"Yes," I answer. "But there are things you can do—get her involved in sports, ballet, children's theater, reading—whatever she's interested in. Help her find a direction for her creativity. She loves writing stories and doing plays. But also give her time to just be Angela. You have a child that most parents would give anything for, Mrs. Gates."

"Maybe you have something there," she smiles, looking relieved. "Look out world, here comes my kid! I'm going to give sports or ballet or the others a try though. And I thought parents with gifted children had it easy."

"Gifted children aren't compliant." I smile. "In fact, they represent the largest challenges a teacher has. They devour knowledge and immediately hunger for more. And as far as creativity, well, I could tell you stories for days," I add emphatically.

"I'll bet none of them ever shaved her eyebrows before," she challenges.

"Want to bet?" I laugh.

Before leaving, she calls Angela from the playground and re-checks her eyebrows. Then she gives her a big hug.

Lord, thank you for the reminder that your gifts sometimes come wrapped in unidentifiable packages. Help me to unwrap every problem with the anticipation that in it I will find your blessing.

CONSIDER IT PURE JOY, MY BROTHERS, WHENEVER YOU FACE TRIALS OF MANY KINDS, BECAUSE YOU KNOW THAT THE TESTING OF YOUR FAITH DEVELOPS PERSEVERANCE (JAMES 1:2–3).

CAUGHT IN MAGGIE'S WEB

*T*hough I have seen very little of Maggie this year, I've seen enough to know that her teaching still varies from nearly brilliant to unbelievably bad.

For example, one day she put up white butcher paper on all her bulletin boards, made black letters, and labelled them all "generic." They stayed that way for three months. Peggy finally must have said something to her. For the next two months there was nothing on them at all. But apparently none of her students suffer from this so-called deprivation. They are as happy and as carefree as their teacher. Some people seem to be loved for what they are rather than what they do, and Maggie is one of them—a real person.

"One thing's for sure. Maggie is a spritely saint," I say to Shelly this morning when the conversation turns to how little I've seen of her this year.

"But she hasn't asked you to travel through Eastern Europe with her this summer," Shelly replies. "You can afford to be generous."

"She's going to Europe this summer?" I ask.

"Yes, she's going through all the Eastern block countries and then on to Scotland."

"To further study the Highland Fling?"

Shelly nods stiffly.

"You don't have to go with her, do you?" I probe.

"No, Pat, I don't *have* to go. And since the last time I told her I definitely wasn't going I've gotten a passport, long thermal underwear, and a new raincoat."

"Shelly," I protest.

"Don't interrupt, Pat," she says in her most teacherly voice. "You've got five kids—no one expects you to go anywhere. Mine are grown. I told Maggie there was no way I would go to Transylvania with her, no way I would meet the few remaining Eastern European gypsies or Czechoslovakian dissidents, and no way I would even learn the Highland Fling. I said all of that in November, December, January, February, March, and April. Now it's May and I'm going."

"Shelly—"

"You keep saying that, Pat. You should know that 'no' is the one word that does not exist in Maggie's vocabulary."

I begin to laugh. I laugh and laugh until tears drip from my chin. "Shelly, you can't really be going to do this!"

"That's what I keep telling myself," she says. "And every week Maggie drops off another list of things to do before the trip. It all just happened," she shrugs. "I'll never know how."

I believe her—Maggie has that kind of effect on people. But I never thought anything like this could happen to good old practical Shelly. "At least you'll do the driving, won't you?" I ask.

"I intend to try," she replies, her eyes getting wide as she remembers riding with Maggie.

"It will be a great trip, Shelly. You deserve to do something special this summer," I say, deciding it's time to give her some support.

"Don't ever say that again, Pat. Why do you think I *deserve* this trip? I'm fifty-one and I want to live to be fifty-two, and yet I let myself be persuaded to take a trip I'd never dream of planning. And

I still don't know how it happened. So much for maturity and wisdom and growing old gracefully."

There's not much more I can say so I don't mention the trip again.

Lord, take care of Shelly. She's such a good friend and good teacher, and I love her. Take care of Maggie, too. She especially needs you, and this school needs at least one good Highland Flinger. But please don't let her drive!

MAY THE LORD KEEP WATCH BETWEEN YOU AND ME
WHEN WE ARE AWAY FROM EACH OTHER
(GENESIS 31:49).

THROUGH EYES OF LOVE

*H*ow I've grown to love these thirty-two little faces. As I mentally compare them to Shelly's class, I wonder how I got all the beautiful children. Hers seem so drab by contrast. But the more I think about it, the more I realize Shelly must feel the same way.

One noon I venture the question. "Do you think your class is more attractive than mine?" I ask her.

"Oh, Pat, I didn't mean for it to be that way," she apologizes. "My kids are just all beautiful this year."

"Know something, Shelly? It's my class that's beautiful. I was just feeling sorry for you!"

"It's love, I guess," she replies. "Once you love you never see people the same way again."

I nod. "The children get more beautiful each day. And one day it's time to say good-bye, to let them go, and to give them time to grow with someone else."

"Every year I cry," Shelly admits. "Because every year I have the best class yet."

"And next year we'll get the worst class of all in September—"

"And turn them into the best by May," she laughs.

Lord, thank you for the change that love has made. And in September, when I have the worst class yet, help me to remember this moment!

LOVE IS PATIENT, LOVE IS KIND. IT DOES NOT ENVY, IT DOES NOT BOAST, IT IS NOT PROUD. IT IS NOT RUDE, IT IS NOT SELF-SEEKING, IT IS NOT EASILY ANGERED, IT KEEPS NO RECORD OF WRONGS (1 CORINTHIANS 13:4–5).

THE END

*I*t's over for another year.

Juan hugs me and whispers, "You're the best teacher I ever had."

Suzanne cries and brings me a picture of a butterfly. Angela brings me one of her stories. Denny is at his seat working— *that's a large enough gift, Lord.*

And Jason, dear Jason, is reading *The Hardy Boys*. "It's a whole series, Mrs. Fisher. It will take all summer at least," he announces with satisfaction.

Patricia still takes out her birthday cards, now in shreds, and hugs them to her, her huge brown eyes lost in remembrance.

Michael saves his comments for share time. "Heather can crawl; you should see her. And I'm not supposed to say this out loud." He leans over and whispers to me, "Dad ordered lots of lice shampoo for next year—and combs, too. Mom said to tell you."

Javier has new shoes, real new ones from the local discount store. "I'm really going to stay out of puddles with these," he announces proudly. Since it won't rain in the Valley for six months, there is some expectation for success.

As they leave the classroom for the last time, I feel tears of both joy and sorrow—joy because I've learned to love these thirty-two little ones; sorrow because I'll miss them and there will never be a class exactly like this one. But it is joy that prevails, and I wonder if every teacher hears the strains of the *Hallelujah Chorus* on the last day of school.

Lord, thank you for the gift of these moments with your youngest saints—even when it rained at recess!

IT IS GOOD TO PRAISE THE LORD AND MAKE MUSIC TO YOUR NAME, O MOST HIGH, TO PROCLAIM YOUR LOVE IN THE MORNING AND YOUR FAITHFULNESS AT NIGHT, TO THE MUSIC OF THE TEN-STRINGED LYRE AND THE MELODY OF THE HARP (PSALM 92:1).